A  **ce**

Also by Tom Douglas

A Theory of Groupwork Practice

Tom Douglas

MACMILLAN

First published 1993 by
THE MACMILLAN PRESS LTD
Houndmills, Basingstoke, Hampshire RG21 2XS
and London
Companies and representatives
throughout the world

ISBN 0-333-54873-6 hardcover
ISBN 0-333-54874-4 paperback

A catalogue record for this book is available
from the British Library.

10   9   8   7   6   5   4   3   2
03   02   01   00   99   98   97   96   95

Printed in Hong Kong

To Shirley, as ever, for her love and constant support

Contents

List of Tables

Preface

This book attempts to address one principal issue and one secondary issue: (1) to provide a common theoretical structure for all forms of groupwork practice, and (2) to make a primary comment about the perplexing and often misunderstood problem of influence. The first is based upon either the idea of a common thread which runs through everything that groupworkers do, or, what often amounts to the same thing seen from a different viewpoint, to accept that some ideas, concepts, principles and so on are bigger, more global in scope than others and can thus contain within their general structure many ideas and practices which have arisen and are used in an independent and sometimes apparently competitive form. In either case the aim is to provide a *theory of practice* (what groupworkers do) which is comprehensive, logical and useful, but which does not seek to replace loyalty to specific theoretical approaches, but rather to clarify the relationship of these to a larger and logical whole.

The second and minor (in this context) issue derives from the need to make it explicit that there is no such thing as a value-free intervention technique even if that technique is apparently based upon so-called 'non-intervention'. What is at issue is not 'to be or not to be' interventionist, but how much, in what way, with what consequences and above all with what intent any form or pattern of groupwork operates.

The Heisenberg Principle of Uncertainty states that ultimate facts continually recede. Thus to expose the influence systems which operate in groupwork promotes the idea that such influences should be made visible because it is not possible to operate without them. But underlying that idea is a value (or values) which accepts that such openness is essential and underneath or behind that lies another set of values which is concerned with the manner of dealing with other human beings and so on.

So, knowing this to be the case (and this knowing is one of the stages in the process), one is forced into accepting the 'As If' syndrome, as in 'I know there are more factors involved but in this case I will act as if there were not.' Thus the factor of importance is 'choice' – what can be accepted as the appropriate cut-off point. There are no certainties, though most of us act 'as if' there were, often at inappropriately 'high' levels of cut-off.

The continuum of leadership is not therefore one which ranges from directive to non-directive, but one in which the application of influence takes different forms, producing different consequences, but, it is hoped, always with the same basic intent – the development or increase of choice and self-responsibility amongst those to whom it is directed.

TOM DOUGLAS

1

Introduction

> This, in part, is why small group theory, social psychology and group dynamics have so little to contribute to the practice and theory of social groupwork ... [They have] ... never come to grips with the empirical gestalt composed of a social group-worker mindful of certain values (those of the agency) and a collection of individuals who are in a special relationship with the worker and with whom the worker is trying to form a group. (Rosenthal, 1973, p. 60)

Rosenthal argues that only by the use of two different kinds of theory, prescriptive and descriptive, can the major aspects of groupwork practice be encompassed. This is a statement which will require careful scrutiny later but for the present it is significant to note that Rosenthal is one of very few commentators on group-work who does not confuse what might be termed theories of human behaviour with theory which is solely concerned with the practice of groupwork. In many texts entitled in one form or another 'groupwork theory' what is offered is distillations of some theory about the way human beings behave plus what are, in effect, principles of practice. In most cases the latter are merely a guideline to an interpretation of group members' behaviour based more or less firmly on a preferred theory and prescriptions for group leader behaviour founded in practice experience but often only tenuously or tangentially connected to the original theory.

What is most interesting here is that these principles of practice are often extremely effective and, because their connection with theory is essentially very tenuous, it follows that they derive their usefulness from being based upon some very simple understanding derived from practice and experience. Thus that which has tended to be regarded as a lesser form of knowledge in comparison to the 'great' theories of human behaviour has in fact been the major contributor to any form of groupwork that has been, and is, effective.

So it becomes necessary to redefine the vast amount of knowledge which is available to groupworkers in a rather clearer and more practical way than heretofore. Initially this may be best displayed as a rather simple chart (Table 1.1), the parts of which may then be examined in some detail.

Ideas about human behaviour and belief systems

By indiscriminate reference to 'theory', 'principle', 'concept' we have avoided stylistic monotony at the expense of clarity and consistency. This has prevented us distinguishing between theorising about practice and the practical implications of theories, as well as between different kinds of theories. (Timms, 1959, p. 172)

In one sense the whole of the systematised knowledge of human behaviour is available to the groupworker. Of course some of it appears to be more relevant and some is certainly more appealing to the individual worker, but however such material is selected the problem of translation is great and that of applicability likewise. A third difficulty lies in the appropriateness of the theoretical concepts used:

a refusal to have one's mental horizon bound by a preoccupation with immediate utility is one thing, while a contrived general irrelevance to all practical problems is quite another; and nothing can be said in favour of the second. (Andreski, 1974, p. 124)

Thus, as the material which has often been called 'borrowed' is seldom produced with a conscious intent that it shall have direct practical applicability, large, undigested and often only partially understood chunks have been accepted into practice.

Writing about what they called the 'major orientations' which influenced work in group dynamics (which is itself well removed

Table 1.1 *Sources*

	Theories: psychological sociological philosophical physical	Statistical	Social organisation management	Mechanics of groups Group dynamics	Values Ethics
Ideas about human behaviour					
Belief systems	The black box syndrome constructs can be formed and used as explanation	Counting creates patterns	Relationships of parts of organisation can be charted and understood	Groups produce consistent observable processes	People can be changed People change themselves Self-determination Democratic ideals: respect for individuals; acceptance; confidentiality; individualisation
Ideas about purposes of working with people in groups	Support; change; empowerment; democratisation; learning; understanding; treatment; growth; actualisation; recreation, etc.				
Action	Techniques for working with people in groups Observation; virtually any selected human behaviour which can be used to remove or diminish obstacles to the emergence and use of the available resources; promotion of the beneficent use of those resources				
Statements about working with people in groups	Case studies; records; research; principles; models; theories of practice; descriptions; areas of practice; applications of theory; innovations; history; groupwork education				

from actual practice with groups), Cartwright and Zander (1953) listed the following eight categories:

1. field theory,
2. interaction theory,
3. systems theory,
4. sociometry,
5. psychoanalytic theory,
6. general psychology,
7. empiricist statistical orientation,
8. formal models orientation.

To these can be added the many developments in branches of psychology such as social psychology, of management studies, organisational studies and so on. It would seem that most areas of study about human behaviour have, quite naturally, yielded some evidence of group behaviour. From these sources groupwork practitioners and theorists have sought to extract information on various aspects of group behaviour. A primary and incomplete list of such borrowings would contain most of the following material: attitudes, authority, communication, composition, conformity, contract, constraints, cohesion, development, decision making, deviance, dyads, embedding, effects of social difference, feedback, individual properties, interaction, intervention, leadership, membership, member satisfaction, motivation, measurement, norms and standards, open/closed groups, observation, power, personal space, performance, prejudice, roles, size, status, subgroups, structure, tasks and values.

What these extracts would all seem to have in common is that they are based upon observation. In essence they constitute a natural history of group behaviour. It might be expected that some observations made by observers of different disciplines would show marked similarities in what is recorded and that others would show extreme difference, and this is essentially true. A simple example of similarity should suffice to illustrate this point. Virtually all writers on group behaviour at some time or other refer to the effect upon group progress and process of the number of members a group contains. Their conclusions are similar despite the differences of descriptive language. But in truth they are statements of the obvious: for example, a large group contains more resources than a small one but the general intensity of relationships within it is lower than in a small group; there are more choices, more places to hide in a large group; and so on.

There are other problems with this material than the generally simplistic nature of the information it contains: (1) the observer effect, (2) the settings effect, (3) the nature and purpose of the observed group, and (4) the extrapolation effect.

The observer effect: all observers of any kind of group have some effect on the group they study in one or more of several different ways:

- intrusive – group members are aware of an alien presence and modify their behaviour accordingly;
- integrated – if an observer is part of the group rather than an external intruder, then his observations are contaminated by the influence of that membership state;
- biased – all observers have expectations of what they will see and/or feel and a specific vocabulary with which to describe their observations;
- speculative – from whatever position an observer cannot in any circumstances have available to him everything that the group is doing, so some degree of speculative infill is natural.

The settings effect: naturally occurring groups are very difficult to observe and the observer effect is correspondingly much greater. Thus most observation of groups is done in 'artificial' groups which have been created for specific purposes, often for the *most* specific purpose of being observed. The awareness of the members of such a group about what is happening must contribute something to their performance.

The nature and purpose of the observed group: this has similarities to the settings effect, but serves to re-emphasise the fact that a large proportion of the data which comprise the natural history of group behaviour is extracted from groups set up precisely for the purpose of experimentation and observation and which otherwise have no existence. The degree of artificiality inherent in all 'created' groups is thus compounded.

The extrapolation effect: because hard data about groups are so difficult to obtain, information derived from one particular source is extrapolated to essentially different settings and used as the

basis of explanation and as the foundation for techniques of intervention. An ameliorating factor in this area is that the general
coarse similarities of all human groups diminish what otherwise
would probably be inapt applications of data.

Kadushin (1959) gave a somewhat different version of the problems of borrowed knowledge:

1. The movement of knowledge between disciplines is liable to
    create the probability of using 'yesterday's knowledge' rather
    than today's.
2. There is the likelihood of endowing borrowed knowledge with
    a greater degree of certainty than its originators would claim
    for it.
3. There is also the probability that the version borrowed has
    been simplified and is thus to that degree falsified.
4. There is the danger that the borrowed material will remain
    undigested, unintegrated and probably unused.

The basic thesis here is not that this material, because of the
problems it entails, is useless; quite the contrary. What is at issue is
the need for the nature and quality, which are often treated as
being of the first order, of this material to be truly appreciated. We
are thus discussing the nature of the thinking about group behaviour which in effect should give a clue to the quality; that is, the
reliability in use of this kind of data:

> as thinking is a deliberate reorganisation of experience and
> behaviour, then logic is a systematic formulation of the pro-
> cedures of thinking that enables this reconstruction to go on
> more economically and more efficiently. (Bolton, 1976, quoting
> Dewey, 1921)

Some of the data presumably have a high probability of being
almost universally applicable and some, however enticing, may
have such a specific relevance that their general applicability is
almost zero. The middle areas of probability may well be available
only as cautious guidelines.

The other major category of borrowed information is formed by
the large theories of human behaviour. In essence they are all
speculative explanations or interpretations of behaviour and in no

way qualify to be regarded as 'facts' which are verifiable in some absolute way. They are constructs which have the value of imposing an element of coherence upon complex observable data.

The data discussed (previously) are, as was stated, descriptive, based upon observation of actually occurring events and essentially stopping at the point of recording or probably at making comparisons with other recorded observations. However such recording has never really provided satisfactory data, so the statement, 'this is what happened', leads into the query, 'why?', which almost always follows. But there is no reliable observable evidence of causation, only attempts to speculate on the probable cause. This is not to be dismissive of such attempts at explanation, but merely to assert their quality, in the same fashion as the observable data were assessed. Such theories have indeed proved worthwhile in helping the development of the understanding of behaviour by providing an elegant structure onto which such observed data as are available will fit without distortion. There is also the predictive factor. Good theories of behaviour should enable behaviour to be predicted. Again there are problems which lie mainly in the area of self-fufilling prophecies.

Once again there is the necessity to assess very carefully the nature and quality of the data which are accepted as the basis for understanding and working with groups. As in some instances it is necessary to teach people a vocabulary to be able to express what is happening to them, I believe that these theories of behaviour present groupworkers with a language and a structure, coherent and often elegant, to use in their attempts to understand what is happening in groups. The fallacious assumption that such theories possess the verifiable factual nature of physical laws is the greatest danger in their use.

Counting the frequency of occurrences and the statistical analysis of such cumulative data can create probability scales of such events happening. This, in some ways the simplest and yet most complex form of situational analysis, is subject to some of the problems already outlined. The process itself is unquestionably objective, but the definition and distinction of what is counted are not. Thus to say that a number of verbal interchanges took place in a given time between noted group members is one thing; to divide those interchanges into categories of intent or even of quality is an entirely different and much more contentious process.

However such counting, allowing for definitional difficulties, does tend to show patterns of behaviour. Given the fact that some form of historical sequential record is kept, then the occurrence of such patterns and the consequences they entail – and their antecedents – may well enhance understanding of what is happening in a rather more 'group' sense than in an 'individual member' sense.

Most of what has just been noted applies to the categories of ideas about human behaviour in Table 1.1. But some special consideration has to be given to the category of values. As I hope to show later, the values which are held by any worker with groups constitute a major influence on what happens in his groups and also on what is recorded as happening. McLeod and Meyer (1967), in a study of the values of social workers, created what they called the 'value dimensions' of social work:

> We have used the notion of dimension rather than position since each value is viewed as a continuum with poles representing contrasting positions held within our society or by some segment of the population. (p. 402)

They suggested that both ends of each continuum were held to be 'legitimate or acceptable to some degree' by social workers. The difference between social work values and those of the general population related mainly to the influence of professional training and to some extent to 'background characteristics'. In that sense they were prepared to accept that social workers may hold distinctive values as a professional group.

The CCETSW Paper 13 of 1976, *Values in Social Work*, listed the following main categories: respect for persons, self-determination, acceptance, confidentiality and individualisation. More importantly the paper presented evidence of value contradictions which existed in different areas of the borrowed knowledge which comprises a large area of the education and training of social workers. If the values of the profession, that is social work, are in conflict to some degree with the values of the disciplines which contribute to the knowledge base, then some amount of confusion no doubt ensues. This problem will be discussed later in the section on the assumptions of groupwork, so it must suffice to say here that a possible remedy for the confusion would be an attempt to make the values which underlie action to be made not only explicit but also visible.

This emerges quite clearly as a necessity when we consider that much training in techniques takes place without any introduction to the theoretical concepts which underpin such techniques or, more importantly, to the value system which is implicit in such concepts. As far back as 1956 this problem was recognised by Gertrude Wilson, who wrote:

> if enablers in groups are trained in techniques without under-standing the principles and basic concepts from which they are drawn, such training raises the floodgates for streams of 'manipulation' rather than 'enabling' people to participate in decision-making processes which safeguard their rights of self-determination. (p. 150)

Ideas about purpose

> Professionals read each other's works and borrow ideas across institutional boundaries. When new ideas such as Gestalt therapy or Transactional analysis are promoted, practitioners from all disciplines hear of them through books and workshops and seek to utilise what they have learned. Clearly then, no set of techniques fully distinguishes any profession's work with groups, and goals and methods overlap. (Garvin, 1981, p. 12)

In considering the ideas which could be seen to derive from sources outside groupwork itself, Garvin listed eleven major approaches and the contributions they could make (see Table 1.2). He ends his statement of approaches with a comment on the similarities of purpose:

> All approaches to groupwork incorporate the professional pur-poses of preventing breakdown of social functioning, providing resources to meet human needs, and rehabilitating individuals whose functioning has been impaired. (p. 23)

Each of the approaches listed in Table 1.2 has developed a set of techniques (shown briefly in the list) with which to achieve its

Table 1.2   *Contributions from sources outside groupwork*

Approach	Purpose	Technique
Gestalt therapy	awareness creation to 'own' beliefs and feelings	by attention to body language; role play of dreams, fantasies and attitudes
Transactional analysis	to discover the effect of ego states	games and scripts
Psychoanalytic group therapy	examination of reaction to common ideas and emotions and therapist conflict between need and fear of consequence	interpretation to engender conflict resolution
Tavistock approach	to disclose basic assumptions to which members are operating	worker inactivity and refusal to assume leader role
Guided group interaction	to describe peer group social processes which determine behaviour	development of a problem terminology, reshaping group norms by confrontation and manipulation
Self-help groups	development of interpersonal support	support, acceptance, enhancing self-esteem by helping others
Psychodrama	to disclose the public aspects of behaviour	confrontation in dramatic role playing of actual behaviour
Behaviour modification in groups	precise goal definition, measurement of progress	application of the principles of conditioning
T-groups	learning about 'how to learn' re interpersonal behaviour	here-and-now focus – feedback in reaction – attention to group process
Social change movements	promotion of a social ideal	empowerment and support
Encounter movement	to engender values of spontaneity, honesty and validity	encouragement of direct emotional expression; physical exercise

purposes and which are in keeping with the basic theoretical orientation of each approach. In essence they are all attempts to remove, diminish or bypass those obstacles, personal, situational and material, which inhibit the use of the existing resources and the development of latent potential.

Much of the theoretical material available to groupworkers is that which is concerned with either the interpretation of behaviour or with the analysis of the dynamics of groups as systems. Thus in the first instance ideas are imported from the psychologies of human b aviour concerned to provide a level of understanding of that observable behaviour, usually on an individual basis, though less frequently in a form which treats the group as an entity. In the second instance the ideas originate in the study of systems and organisations and are concerned with interrelational structures, energy and outcomes.

Even in Gestalt psychology, where the basic unit of concern is the group and its leaders, the concepts available are on a level of theorising which is, to say the least, somewhat distant from the nitty-gritty of actual groupwork. The point taken as central here is that people choose to work with groups as a preferred form of service delivery and that this work has been in existence long enough for it to have produced sufficient evidence, albeit diverse and diffuse, of the ubiquitous nature of certain elements. Thus these common elements of work with groups, whatever the starting-point in terms of wider theoretical orientation, can form that basis of a theory of practice – that is, a coherent account of what people who work with groups actually do – and ultimately provide a theory of practice which is universally applicable.

Action

> The relationship between knowing and doing has as many puzzles for us today as it had for Socrates. Indeed, all of psychology is involved with it in one way or another. (Blanton, 1962, p. 10)

As this area of groupwork is covered in greater detail in Chapter 6, it should suffice here to indicate the sandwich position the stratum labelled 'action' occupies in Table 1.1.

Basically the ideas in the first three strata represent some of the material available to groupworkers and which they can use to underpin their practice. But inevitably practice produces experience of how things were achieved or not and in time this leads to the production of material which is in essence a record of that experience. Thus the actions, decisions and techniques of groupworkers are fed both by ideas from other disciplines and by material derived from the records of actual practice – as it were by information from before and after practice has taken place. Somewhere in this feed-in process from both sides lies the great problem of translation and adaptation referred to by Blanton above. In the very simplest approach, and probably the best, ideas from both sides have to be tried out, monitored and adopted or discarded. Because one of the major elements of groupwork is the groupworker, the most effective practice has to be founded upon ideas and the development of techniques which are to a very great extent compatible with the kind of person who will use them. This should not preclude knowledge and understanding of ideas which reside outside the individual groupworker's conception of compatibility. But such empirical testing should be the basis of individual practice.

There is one area of the practice of groupwork where the connection between knowledge and action is very clear and precise. This lies in the area of group creation or adaptation and to a lesser extent in the process which has come to be known as 'holding'. Nothing is more certain than that the efficacy of the process of beginning in groupwork is dependent upon the knowledge which the groupworker possesses about the dynamics of groups, the structures of which they are composed and the relationship of these factors to the amount of time necessary to achieve them. Indeed this knowledge is akin to the ability to prophesy. Thus the groupworker's knowledge should be adequate to the planning and the carrying forward of a group at a time when others, that is, group members, may well be devoid of any real concept of what is to be expected or possible. This is the time, as we shall discuss later, when an incipient system needs a large energy input, a starter, which has to come from the worker, before perception of what may be gained from the group serves to increase commitment and thus energy input from the members of the group.

This area of action, then, that is related to the beginning stage, is much different from the actions which follow, that is those related to the ongoing process of the group. This difference is marked by the fact that most of the attempts to formulate a theory of groupwork practice have been concentrated here and faded away or ignored later developments. I think that the issue may not be just one of clarity of the relationship of knowledge to practice but also one of explicit control. Most groupwork texts are written for groupworkers and thus are concerned with leadership acts and intervention. It follows from this that, in the area where such behaviour is absolutely appropriate, formulation of theory becomes relatively easy.

Statements about work with groups

The material included in this category was well documented by Silverman (1966), who listed sources of information about group-work which came from practitioners as revealed in the literature (Table 1.3). From these statements the principal areas of what might be called 'pure' groupwork knowledge have been derived. A matter of some concern is the possible misinterpretation of the

Table 1.3 *Sources of information about groupwork*

1	Descriptions	of work in progress or completed
2	Areas of practice	work in particular settings or with specific client groups
3	Appeals for knowledge	the exposure of deficiencies in groupwork knowledge and appeals for systematising of existing knowledge
4	Appeals for direction of service	attempts to persuade workers to adopt an interest in specific programmes
5	Traditional statements of principles	practical guidelines and ethical prescriptions based on professional values
6	Applications of social science	the attempted application of selected themes and concepts in some aspects of groupwork
7	Innovations in practice theory	reformulations of practice theory in attempts to provide guidelines for groupwork activity
8	Research and surveys	general testing of hypotheses and data collection in given areas
9	Groupwork– casework–group therapy	comparisons of groupwork with 'clinical' orientations
10	Historical articles	groupwork in historical perspective
11	Social groupwork	the education and training of groupworkers

descriptive term 'pure', for the simple reason that, although groupwork knowledge defined by it comes from recorded practice, the practice itself has been influenced by the attitudes and concepts of the practitioners and of the organisations for which they work.

Let us take a simple example, that of the developmental sequences which have been so frequently recorded. Initially the sequence was described lineally: state B followed state A and in turn was followed by state C. Then various elaborations were introduced which replaced the lineal development pattern with ones which were not only progressions but also included regressions, repetitions and indeed plateaux and stagnation. In some ways the developmental sequence of groups became similar in generating expectations of the stages to be reached and passed and of what those stages should contain as the human growth and development sequences of childhood maturation. The latter, however, were much less dependent for their fulfilment upon the beliefs and expectations of parents than were the former upon the beliefs of groupworkers.

Of course there tends to be a pattern of familiarisation in groups which is directly related to time of exposure of members to one another. But it is also related to so many other factors which are not so apparent, for instance, past experience, personal characteristics and preceptions. The utility of practice-derived information lies absolutely in the provision of what might be described as a sketch map. It is not, and cannot be, a precise ordnance survey. Such information must deal in probabilities, not anywhere near a high order of certainty, but providing signposts and guidelines. The similarities in group development are indeed great, but the probability of difference is also great, if not in sequence at least in timing and in intensity. Each group is a balance between the uniqueness it generates from the difference of its members and its situation and its similarity to all other groups which stems from the patterns of influence of members, groupworkers and organisations grounded in conformity and commonality.

The major problem of these practice-derived items of knowledge would seem to lie, with certain exceptions, in their lack of comparability. So the cumulative whole is a collection of relatively individual items with but few common threads serving to unite them into larger wholes. This means that in effect practitioners have a wide-ranging choice of what to use, a selection almost entirely directed by personal preference and not by proven worth.

There are, however, areas of this practice-derived knowledge which have become statements of principles, descriptions of the way in which borrowed ideas and information have functioned in practice, as well as ideas drawing directly on some specific area of practice. Ultimately there are also attempts to formulate in a given structure some form of larger statement about groupwork such as is to be found in the formation of models: 'A model is a conceptual design to solve a problem that exists in reality . . . [and which] orders those elements in a given universe that are relevant to solve the problem' (Pappell and Rothman, 1966). Models of groupwork have arisen as practitioners and others have tried to discover what if any logical relationships exist between what Pappell and Rothman call a 'guiding consensus' and the pragmatic 'hands-on' solutions to tasks which groupworkers have produced in practice. They are, in essence, attempts to make sense of complex real situations in a way that will stand transfer and extrapolation with undiminished value.

The formulations by Pappell and Rothman and most others since have been based upon function and/or focus and in this sense they are basically problem-oriented. For instance, given a number of people with a particular problem, what kind of group could be used to focus on a particular aspect of the problem? The difficulty for groupworkers with models like this is that, because of the lack of alternative sources in the process of providing help and understanding of group situations, they will be translated into concrete factual data. As Pashley (1967) says of the worker: 'From being useful tools to assist him in the interpretation of his observations they could become the agents of hard and fast prescription' (p. 13). To realise the limitations of models is to recognise that it is a fallacy to assume that to achieve an accepted paradigm of the dynamics of small groups is even possible:

> Any unity that may be achieved will not be by insisting upon a universally accepted paradigm but by acknowledging the various aspects of the Weltanschauungs that have played a part in structuring our views of the dynamics of small groups. Thus what unity we may find will be a function of the question we ask. (Boyd, 1991, p. 14)

Aims of the book

The belief that it is possible to make generalisations above the
level of experiencing is the first major step in developing a
climate in which social work theories can be made and exciting
models can be built. (Schwartz, 1963, p. 45)

Schwartz went on to add that practitioners need theories indicating
that the lack of them creates immense problems of integration. I
would add that without some systematisation the possibility of
making comparisons of material from many sources becomes
remote. This is important because it is by compilation and by
direct comparison that out of the vast welter of data emerge the
constants which form the bases of, first, lists of principles, then
models and, finally, complete theories. Schwartz points out that
'scientism' – the idea that knowledge comes to its own 'implications for practice' is a fallacy. The mere accumulation of data of
itself does not provide ideas for action without the conscious
application of analysis, comparison and structure. Again to quote
Schwartz, 'it is more a dynamic process of interaction, in which
each plays its hunches into the other, each feeds on the other's
experiences'. The essential link is that of purpose and, as we shall
see later, purpose arising from beliefs and values is a crucial
shaping factor in groupwork.

Thus the aim of this book can be stated very simply and precisely:
*to present a coherent theory of groupwork which will inform and
integrate the practice of working with people in groups.* As the
previous sections of this introductory chapter have amply demonstrated, the amount of material available to groupworkers is vast,
so to approach the aim of this book from the back, as it were, it
should be said that it is *not* an attempt to add to the plethora of
existing theories of group behaviour.

It is our aim to try to show that all forms of working with groups
of people, no matter how different in ideological approach, are
essentially working with the same basic factors and in fact *doing*
the same things however described or disguised. Thus another way
of defining the aim of this book is to say that it is an attempt to
define those basic factors, purposes and actions, in the simplest
possible way without distortion and to generate a structure which
integrates them in a defined relationship.

In the baldest of manners this aim can be stated as follows:

1. to show that all groupwork follows a very simple pattern:
   - recognise need and analyse it;
   - define or redefine individuals as groups;
   - create a unit/system which will offer facilities for (a) the location of resources (actual and potential), (b) such resources to be made available, (c) such resources to be used for the group (and maybe others also), (d) monitoring the consequences of such use;
   - terminate or transform the group;
   - assess and evaluate the outcomes.
2. to show that all members of a group (including leaders) bring resources into it (actual and potential) which include their networks of past and current contacts, knowledge, experience and so on.
3. to show that 'directive' leadership is the dominance of one or more particular resource systems and that 'facilitative' leadership is a process of developing access to as many resource systems as possible within and outside the group system.
4. to offer brief illustrative material to show how these basic and integrated theoretical concepts are adopted in practice.

In essence the theory to be presented here is in some ways a statement of the obvious. Its value is to demonstrate that groupworkers should apply infinitely more energy and attention to the creation and use of the units of resource they create (that is groups) than they do now to the interpretation of behaviour and that the ultimate appropriateness of such action can be measured in terms of consequence.

2

Interactive and Affiliative Patterns in Groups

As far as we know, Aristotle was the first person to formulate basic principles of social influence and persuasion; but, although he did say that man is a social animal, he was probably not the first person to make that observation. Moreover, chances are he was not the first person to marvel at the truth of that statement while simultaneously puzzling over its triteness and insubstantiality. (Aronson, 1980, p. 1)

Nor can such conceptions as individual, personality, self, or mind be described except in terms of membership in a group or groups – unless again we wish to hug the figment of the individual as a detached, self-contained entity. (Malinowski, 1939, p. 938)

In any serious attempt to understand the processes of groupwork it is essential to start with some discussion of why groups, created or adapted, have become such a widespread and effective method of responding to a large range of human problems and activities.

In a very simplistic sense the answer is obvious. Designed groups are a conscious adaptation of a universally pre-existing 'natural' phenomenon, but this fact has been obscured in two particular ways. The first is that existence in some form of group is such a universal and ubiquitous experience that, like the air we breathe, it is accepted to the point of oblivion. It surfaces as a matter to be considered, like the air, only when a crisis concerning it forces it into our conscious thinking. The second way is that investigation into human behaviour, as Henriques *et al.* (1984) say,

' "neglected" the social world, and was unable to bridge the individual–society divide. . .'.

The concentration upon the individual, which may, as many have suggested, be little more than an abstraction, has without doubt delayed and constricted the development of understanding of the social nature of human existence.

Man as a social animal – or why we need others

Deep within every man there lies the dread of being alone in the world, forgotten by God, overlooked among the tremendous household of millions and millions. That fear is kept away by looking upon all those about one who are bound to one as friends or family, but the dread is nevertheless there and one hardly dares think of what would happen to one of us if all the rest were taken away. (Kierkegaard, in Dru, 1938)

The experiments in social isolation and sensory deprivation seem to have confirmed the idea that the presence of others, either in actuality or in the imaginative projection of a previously experienced reality (the Robinson Crusoe pattern), is essential to the maintenance of mental and physical health and stability. There is little need here to dwell on the process of maturation, or indeed on the fact that most human beings spend a considerable proportion of their working life and leisure time in groups of one sort or another, with different degrees of 'belonging' and of commitment. But there is some need to restate some of the other consequences of that fear of isolation so graphically described by Kierkegaard in his journals. Raven and Rubin (1976) list some of these consequences in terms of needs: (1) the need for love and approval, and as (a) physical rewards – sustenance, warmth; (b) liking – approval, companionship, love; (c) affiliation and fear reduction; (2) the need to be provided with information about our world and about ourselves, for example via comparisons – of abilities, opinions and feelings. They go on to say, 'Because of the fact that we need others for direct satisfaction of our needs and for information about our environment and its meaning, we are uniquely vulnerable.' This vulnerability, they maintain, this dependence upon others, means that we are open to being significantly influenced by others. In very direct terms this would seem to indicate that not only do we need others as a major support of mental and physical stability, but also that the way, the manner in which that support is obtained and from whom, shapes and influences our central behaviour patterns.

It would therefore seem logical that, as indeed has occurred, such powerful influencing agents as groups are used to effect change both in individuals and in the systems in which they live, to support, to enhance learning and to act as generators of power. All these factors are already essential to and discoverable in groups and groupings which occur in the ordinary course of human existence.

Bonner (1959) indicated that what he called 'basic and derived needs' could only be accommodated through the co-operation of others, that 'survival, security, friendship, affection and the like can only be gratified in groups'. If these sources of power, influence and support are to be used and applied, as it were, at the point of most need with conscious and deliberate intent, then we are faced with the somewhat hazardous task of analysing what actually happens in the so-called natural groups and then of translating the results into a series of skills, methods, techniques and understandings for use in the groups we create or adapt.

Much research has been carried out over the past fifty or so years into the dynamics of groups (see Chapter 1), the behaviour of individuals in groups and of course into the adaptation of many different kinds of pre-existing theories of human behaviour to the develpment of forms of groupwork. But it is a long, hard road from the analysis of groups as instruments for the gratification of certain reasonably well-defined needs to the realisation of the nature of the skills and competencies required to establish groups designed to meet the needs of all those to whom such a process of group formation would never occur. In this sense, although it is obvious that naturally occurring groups succeed, the problem is to know why and how.

Perhaps the simplest point should be made first, which is that there are many things that human beings wish to do which can only be accomplished by several people acting in concert. It is interesting that this fact should be so readily understood about some activities yet, when the concept of sharing is introduced, often as a reason for creating or adapting a group, many find great difficulty in handling it. Admittedly some of this difficulty is caused by the insidious influence of a society which seems to corner people into the belief that their problems, difficulties and needs are unique and, moreover, their responsibility alone. Thus, although some elements of support are available from the immediate society, many difficulties which may attract the label 'special' are seen as being a purely personal matter.

It is significant that one of the problems of retirement has proved to be the gross diminution of points of contact with others; that is, points of contact defined as those constant affirmations that one is who one has learnt to be – the markers which measure out time in expected quantities. The elderly in old people's homes, reduced to a minimum of social contacts by lack of mobility or other factors, value intensely the routines, like meals, which constitute markers for them, points to look for, and which involve some happening in conjunction with others. They are a reflection of the way in which the need for contact survives. Despite the dilution of social contacts as old age and disability force on people, who are then compelled to retreat into their memories of past experience, such contact points remain high spots in their lives.

Carolyn Sherif (1976) describes what she calls 'social anchors' which amount to the groups, jobs, settings, people and ideas which exist in her life and with which she has a familiar relationship; they act to hold her in her place in her society. These 'networks' will admit of gradual and partial change or elimination without much loss of stability or even with a temporary loss, but when a large and sudden loss of such 'anchors' occurs it greatly enhances the essential fear of isolation and separateness.

It would seem that one thing that human beings cannot do other than together is to ensure their sense of place, their security. Not for nothing has the major punishment of social offenders always included an element of ostracism, of being abandoned, of being isolated from the community. In primitive societies this was often tantamount to a sentence of death. To 'stay in touch' is essential. But, in order to receive the benefit of being 'networked' or 'anchored' in Sherif's meaning, the individual has to be acceptable, at the very least to a limited number of those whom he wishes to join. This is the process of affiliation.

Affiliation

Collins' Concise English Dictionary defines 'affiliate' in this manner: 'to receive into close connection or association (with a larger body, group or organisation etc.); to associate oneself with'. It is a normal part of social life that individuals will attempt to join others to achieve an enormously wide spectrum of satisfaction, ranging all the way from the simple pleasure of being in the company of others, to the most precise role fulfilment in a tightly knit group or team. The necessity of these 'joinings' has never been questioned and they are usually described as being 'natural' in the sense which has already been used here.

Perhaps this highlights the basic difference between 'natural' groups and those which are 'created' for the purpose of groupwork – in a word, the sense that they are the creations of others and therefore that they attract the description of 'artificial'. Any form of so-called artificiality is almost bound to arouse at least some suspicion on the part of probable participants, who would never have such feelings about joining a group of complete strangers in order to learn some skill or technique which they themselves had decided was necessary.

The deeper and more personal the need which is to be met in an 'offered' group the greater probably the anxiety and the suspicion experienced by the potential participants, though there must come levels of desperation in some people's lives where anything is preferable to a continuation of the existing state. It is interesting to note that in some forms of group, as in the treatment of alcoholics and of addicts, this state of desperate lowness is the essential point of departure from which, as the saying goes, 'there is nowhere to go but up'. The process of being accepted, of being permitted to affiliate, is intricately bound up with the concepts of conformity. In fact affiliation to a group or organisation is frequently made conditional on the acceptance of explicit and implicit rules, of norms of behaviour. Probationary periods in more formal organisations and systems are provided both for the newcomer and for the organisation to discover, in the one instance, whether the cost of conforming to the rules and norms is a viable and acceptable outlay for what membership can bring in terms of rewards and, in the other, whether the newcomer can conform and what element, if any, of value, actual or potential, to the organisation, might be available.

Of course people become members of systems involuntarily as well as voluntarily and then other methods of diminishing conflict and confrontation within the system other than absolute willing confirmity become necessary.

Private acceptance/public conformity

It is customary to use the dichotomy private acceptance/public conformity to describe the difference between wholehearted acceptance of the rules and norms of an organisation and all the other forms of survival within it which, in essence, fall short of that total acceptance. Words such as 'compliance', 'deference' and 'obedience' spring to mind to describe behaviour patterns, the basis of which must be the need to survive for a period of time within an organisation with a set of norms which range from being different to being overtly or covertly hostile. This situation carries with it a certain need to convince significant others, significant in the sense of possessing power to exert sanctions, that the rules will be obeyed and the organisational norms observed even though the level of commitment to, and belief in, those rules and norms is minimal or even non-existent. Where initiation into an organisation is part of a voluntary process, then the sense of 'withholding' full commitment, which is characteristic of a public conformity approach, is often temporary and is based upon ignorance and appropriate caution. Until the extent of the costs involved is better known – as practical issues rather than as information which carries an unknown and unexperienced reality behind it – commitment can only be given within the perceived limits of personal safety and acceptable expenditure.

Perhaps what emerges from this is that, where the process of affiliation is to take place and the group to which affiliation is offered does not easily or readily fall into the acceptable category of being 'natural', a barrier of artificiality exists to the exploitation of group processes for the benefit of the individual. Indeed what the examination of 'natural' groups demonstrates with remarkable clarity is that the choice, the selection of a group, the when, how and why to join are of fundamental importance.

The family

The most important group of all, the family of origin, which also conditions future group choices in one way or another, has no entry choices itself. So much has been written about the effects of the family as a group that the barest bones of information should suffice to recall all that is needed for this discussion. The family of origin is the first group we experience and is always the most powerful, if only because it exerts its influence when we are most susceptible and impressionable. It creates the patterns of group response which shape all later responses, even if the original responses are eventually used as the epitome of how not to respond in groups. In essence it sets the basic patterns of influence and response. It also sets the patterns of the ways in which these influences are used. The latter seem to be rather more susceptible to change by the conscious adoption of different patterns in later years than the former. Most of these changes or adaptations seem to be made as a result of the widening spectrum of contacts during the process of growing up and later. Here different ways, different attitudes, opinions, beliefs and behaviour patterns have a chance of superseding the original family conditioning on the basis that reason indicates that the new ways are superior in some apparent sense. The interactions available have increased and variety and difference become fascinating factors.

Interaction

To start once again with a dictionary definition the *Collins' Concise English Dictionary* offers the following: Interact – to act on or in close relation with each other; Interaction – allowing or relating to continuous two-way transfer of information between a user and the central point of a communication system (of two or more persons, forces etc.) acting upon or in close relation with each other; interacting.

Jay M. Jackson (1953), writing about interaction in groups, listed the functions of such behaviour as follows: (1) to provide individual members with social reality concerning others' expectations and evaluations; (2) to reinforce approved behaviour and extinguish disapproval; (3) to attract or repel persons from membership; (4) to maintain the quality of the social system by drawing highly valued members into centrality and by making peripheral or repelling the small contributor. In fact interaction is the essential concept, according to Stogdill (1959), 'for a definition of small groups'. He goes on to say:

> A group may be regarded as an open interaction system in which actions define the structure of the system and successive interactions exert co-equal effects upon the identity of the system.

Those factors which help and encourage, perhaps even generate, interaction must be very wide. But if our ultimate aim is to be able to generate not only general interaction, but interaction deliberately, that is, consciously, introduced to promote specific outcomes, then it is essential that some attempt be made to be more definitive, even if this does appear to be as impossible as measuring the volume of unconfined smoke.

A review of some of the immense volume of literature on interaction would tend to suggest that eight principal generative factors may be distinguished:

1. communication: as communication increases, because it is one of the basic elements of interaction, so the functions listed by Jackson are more likely to develop;
2. perceptions of members of several factors: (a) similarity – this appears to be positively related to interaction (Zander and Havelin, 1960), (b) status – members of a group interact more with those of a higher status (Zalesnik and Moment, 1964), (c) liking – liking may be a function of interaction or interaction a function of liking (Israel, 1956), (d) situation – interaction stems from a definition of the situation (Zalesnik and Moment, 1964);
3. frequency and intensity of exposure;
4. physical and functional proximity;
5. the capacity of group members: (a) inclination, (b) emotional expansiveness, (c) social expansiveness;
6. past experience;
7. need to reinforce approved behaviour;
8. need to provide a social reality.

Such a list, despite its vagueness and its statements in such wide and general terms, immediately serves to reveal that, if the functions of 'normal' groups are to be consciously and selectively used in created groups to obtain desired ends, here is a basic checklist for the promotion of directional interaction in the group. But what are the observable facts of interaction? Another general list may be derived from the literature: interaction (1) generates understanding, (2) spreads information, (3) enhances conformity of opinion, (4) facilitates goal achievement, and (5) generates personal attraction. Of course there are many other factors, both good and bad. For instance, interaction is as likely to generate dislike as liking, depending upon a large number of other influences, such as past experience.

Finally it would be advisable to note any indication of what might influence interactive patterns once they are in existence. A simple list would then contain such factor as:

1. the size of the group – more attention will be paid to this later, but it must be obvious that the larger the group the greater the number of possible interactions, up to some unknown limit;
2. the developmental stage which the group has achieved – it is probably a statement of the obvious to say that familiarity reduces some interaction barriers;
3. structure – in a sense structure defines those members between whom interaction of various kinds is possible and the nature of that interaction, especially in large formal groups;
4. goal achievement – success in the group tasks seems to increase the rate and spread of interaction between group members;
5. group influence – the norms of the group and its rules may well pressurise even the usually reluctant into interaction with others.

Already the parameters of the creation of a group for specific defined ends begin to emerge from what is discoverable about the ways in which 'natural' groups work. But what has been presented here tends to show that, if certain factors are available and present in a group, other factors occur, but there is little in this cause/effect analysis which could answer the question, why? In fact it may be too sanguine to suggest a cause/effect sequence, which has a connotation of a known path of influence, rather than just a sequential relationship as a description of the presented analysis. In most instances what has been recorded has been of the nature of observed consequence and thus of apparent consequence. So how can we answer the question, why? I believe that, at the risk of being repetitive, it is necessary to go back to the starting-point for the only available answer.

Why?

If, as many believe, language defines the manner of our thoughts and in that sense enables us to construct a reality, then language should contain some clue about the position of groups in our reality. In fact this proves to be an apt investigation. Given that the number and variety of words which are widely available and used about a particular human condition will give a rough indication of its importance, then even a cursory glance at a thesaurus will show an interesting fact. There are some 143 nouns of assemblage in Roget. Thus the attempts to find words to describe the ways in which human beings come together for all manner of purposes has produced a plethora of words, and this without the addition of all those words which are of slang, jargon or argot derivation, which would add greatly to the number given here.

Does this lead to an answer to the why question? Does it lead to the idea that man is, as Aristotle said, a social animal; that the natural state of all human beings is as a member of a group or groups and that the intensely individual and personal nature so prized by all is only possible when we are embedded in and supported by such groups, even though the support system may be very hard to read for what it actually is?

It is of little consequence at this stage to ask why human beings are programmed to believe in individuality, though the processes of child-rearing may have something to contribute to the answer. What is important is that human contact, response and feedback are as essential in their way as oxygen or blood.

An African proverb says, 'The earth is a beehive; we all enter by the same door but we live in different cells.' This essential isolation, this separateness has been recognised and commented upon by thinkers for centuries, but the behaviours which counteract the terrifying fear it engenders and their fundamental nature have not been so well covered. But it is precisely these counteractive behaviours which derive from a compelling urge to allay that fear which are the powerful basis of all grouping. Solitude should never be confused with isolation. The former is a chosen state, selected in the knowledge that society exists and that the state of being alone can usually be terminated at will. Isolation is the state into which we are born and the reason why we need to develop the skills, and to receive the comfort and support, of association.

The helplessness of the human infant leaves its lifelong mark; it may be partly responsible for man's ready submission to authority wielded by individuals or groups, his suggestibility by doctrines and commandments, his overwhelming urge to identify himself with tribe or nation, and above all with a system of beliefs. (Arthur Koestler at a meeting of Nobel prizewinners in Stockholm in 1967, speaking on the theme, 'The place of value in a world of facts')

Propositions

1. Man is a social animal.
1a. Because groups have been and are instrumental in creating and in maintaining the individual in all aspects of his life, it is logical that created or adapted groups should be used as the means to support, reshape, educate or change the life style of individuals in a conscious and planned way to beneficial ends.

3

Associative Patterns in Created and Adapted Groups

Why do we need others? Essentially, we need them for the rewards they can offer us and the costs they can help us avoid; we also need others for the information they can provide about our world and about ourselves. (Raven and Rubin, 1976, p. 41)

It seems likely that affiliative social bonds have survival value for groups and that innate affiliative patterns of behaviour have evolved. Relations between members of a group can be seen as an equilibrium between aggression and affiliative processes: the affiliative processes hold the aggressive ones in check. (Argyle, 1970, p. 31)

In order to resolve what might be a confusion between affiliation and association a simple definition would be that affiliation is a need or a drive and associative patterns are the visible products of that drive. Argyle was writing about animals in the quotation given above, but what he was describing in the balance between aggression and the satisfaction of affiliative need is common enough in human groups also. In fact one of the great obstacles to the discovery and use of group resources, as we shall discover later, is the different levels of equilibrium which group members achieve between suspicion and fear of the group and the basic need to be accepted by it. In other words the balance between cost and reward as perceived by the individual is matched exactly by the balance between commitment and the withholding of comitment. As perceptions change so this balance changes to a different level in which one side of the equation has altered in value.

In groupwork groups the associative patterns, unlike those in naturally occurring or non-artificial groups, create a continuum of group-oriented or instrumental patterns to leader-oriented or contextual patterns. This continuum is not a true one; rather it is a pattern of differential dominance often connected with the influence of the group leader or with the assessed needs of the group in a given period of its life.

Essentially these two associative patterns are the ends of this so-called continuum and are approached in various ways in group-work literature. Usually they are dichotomised into opposites on the basis that they are founded upon different concepts of patterns of influence. They are commonly represented as leadership or as leader-oriented/group-oriented, but in each case the point of view is that of how much or how little leader input is desirable.

It should be appreciated, however, that, in terms of the conflict between affiliative drives and fear of power, associative patterns should be established not on the basis of an external approach but logically on the needs of members at any given time and in any given circumstance. Norma C. Lang (1972) came close to an under standing that associative patterns in a group should be related to the capacity and needs of the individual members. She postulated three forms of group, to which she gave the cumbersome titles of allonomous, allon-autonomous and autonomous, meaning in effect leader-directed, mixed and group-directed. But in the process of addressing these three forms Lang also indicated which form was most appropriate for what type of group members. Her assessment was based not simply on the kind of problems which group members might have, nor upon the policy of the organisation for which the group leader worked, nor yet upon the theoretical assumptions of that leader, but upon such factors as the unit to be worked with (group, individual or combination), the focus of service, the levels of social process to be addressed, the nature of the worker role, the nature of the client, the group processes to be dealt with and finally the means by which the goals of the group might be achieved.

The fact that Lang's thesis sought to synthesise what had pre-viously been accepted as different models by demonstrating that they could all be seen as aspects and parts of a larger model (a stochastic theory in effect) appears to have led to her paper having little apparent impact on groupwork theorising. Even more so, her almost secondary assumption that groupwork groups should be established on the basis of the needs, capabilities and experience of the potential members of being able to use groupwork has been ignored.

Referring to her synthesised model, Lang writes, 'the model poses an important relationship between the functioning capacity of the individual and the nature of the resulting entity individuals of a given capacity are able to perform.' We must now look at this triad of group 'forms' in a rather different way.

Instrumental associative patterns

Instrumental associative patterns, or more properly group-as-instrument patterns, appear in a group when the group members are able to work as a unit to explore and exploit the resources which the group contains or to which it has access. Perhaps the most interesting factor about this kind of group historically is the close connection it has always been deemed to have with the concepts of equality and democracy. In truth, such groups seldom just emerge; they need to be created and they often need some considerable time to learn about themselves and the ways in which their resources can be used. For this reason most groups which operate as a unit contain group-sophisticate members, so that the experience of what the benefits of sharing and resource access are likely to be is available for the less group-sophisticate members. The associative patterns here are complex and may best be described as constituting multiple membership of linked sub-groups within the group itself. Overall status may well be very similar, except at times when the specific knowledge and skill of one member are seen to be of greater value to the group in the pursuit of its aims than those of other members.

Because of the length of time necessary for group members to learn about themselves and their resources, the development of a high level of self-governance is often a later stage in a group which starts off with a contextual associative pattern (group-as-context). So, although we are here regarding the group-as-instrument as a separate group associative pattern, it would be more correct to regard it as a definable stage or as a possible objective. Lang (1972) provides a good summary of the major factors relating to this associative pattern:

1. the group is autonomous – self-directing;
2. the group-as-a-whole is the basic work unit;
3. individual activity is directed to achieving group goals;
4. the social process involved is that of the group-as-whole;
5. the nature of the group is mature;
6. the leader's role is facilitative;
7. the group members are capable and skilled;
8. all group processes are dealt with by the leader indirectly to generate increased self-directed behaviour by the group.

As Lang uses a leader-focused approach in her description of what is essentially a group-focus situation, it is not inappropriate to look at another contribution slanted in this way.

> The group-centered leader prefers to adopt as his working hypothesis the belief that the individual has a vast store of untapped potential for positive, constructive, intelligent and mature behavior. (Gordon, 1972)

Gordon goes on to suggest that the way of tapping this potential, what I have consistently referred to here as 'resources', is by what amounts to a transfer of the central power of the leader to the group members. Thus he states that the utilisation of member potential is directly related to those members being liberated from dependence upon the leader or other authority. He maintains that goals must be those set by the group, change must be that initiated by the group, democracy must be maintained by democratic procedures used in an atmosphere which is not threatening, and leadership of the group must be a rotating function of group members, relating to their capacity and willingness to perform in situations for which their known talents are appropriate.

Indeed the group leader in the associative pattern is no less skilled, knowledgeable or powerful than the leader of the contextual group and is therefore equal in being the major resource. But, as we shall see, the aims of such leaders in the use of their abilities is significantly different. The group-as-instrument leader is aiming to use his skills to create a learning situation for group members where ultimately they will be able to take over and run their group for themselves with sufficient knowledge and skill to obtain their objectives. The leader may or may not stay as part of the group when this is achieved, but if he does stay, then his role becomes only one among many leader roles which are based upon matching the demands of a given situation or series of situations with the appropriate and available abilities.

On the other hand, the leader of a group-as-context maintains his position as the single most important available resource during the existence of the group. It is this kind of role function and the associative pattern that goes with it that we must now consider.

Group-as-context associative patterns

In very simple terminology this pattern occurs when the group is the context in which a powerful and knowledgeable resource, usually one leader, operates. There are many models and practices which conform to this pattern, ranging from the concept of the members of a group being siblings with the same parent/child relationship to the group leader, through Redl's concepts of Central Person to the group practice of Perls.

This pattern of association is one in which all group members have a primary relationship to the group leader who works with each individual in turn in the context of the group. The major resource available to the group is the expertise, knowledge and skill of the group leader. But it should never be overlooked that this powerful and immediately available resource needs the use of the resources of the group members to be effective. If, as in the parable, the seed falls upon stony ground, then no crop is forthcoming. Indeed so much has been made in the past of the skill, knowledge and experience of such a leader that inadequate attention has been given to the abilities of the group members to absorb and use what is being offered to them. This absorption has to take place at two different levels: the first when an individual member is engaged directly by the group leader on a one-to-one basis for a period of time, the second when each member of the group is part of the background (the context) in which the one-to-one engagement is taking place. Given that the group members have some identity of problem or reason for being in the group in the first place, what they observe will have direct relevance to them in both the content and the process of the interaction. Consideration of this associative pattern leads directly to speculation about the distinction and difference between dyadic interaction and group interaction (sometimes called 'polyadic'), both of which are apparently features of contextual groups.

> It is quite easy to substantiate empirically that an individual is capable of *genuinely* engaging one and only one other person in total communication in any given moment. (Smith, 1978, p. 293)

If what Smith avers is true, then the difference between the contextual associative pattern's two parts is one of intensity of involvement and focus.

Intensity of involvement varies between that of a total dyadic relationship between the leader and one group member, when the awareness and involvement of the other group members diminishes significantly, but perhaps never to the level of extinction, and a participatory involvement in the dyadic process of some other member of the group and the leader. This second involvement is less intensely focused by the individual member on himself and more intensely focused on what is happening in the group as a whole. Because there is no overtly, actively expressed involvement in the nature of this interchange it is observational in character and its focus has a wider nimbus and a diminished centre of self-focus.

> It is axiomatic and empirically demonstrable that the individual is capable of engaging no more than one person in genuine dialogue – total reciprocity – in an existential moment. This universally human limitation renders the interactional network indispensable to the group process. (Smith, 1978, p. 302)

However, in being so specific in defining communication patterns, Smith appears to ignore the fact that, while communication is generally agreed to be a two-way process and interaction likewise, there is still the process of one addressing several where the interaction is one of attention and interest and where the feed-back which would establish the response leg of this two-way process may be delayed or indeed never be available. It is equally possible that interaction between the whole group or even some sub-group and the leader can take place at the level of feeling which, despite its possible vagueness of focus, could be quite powerful.

Ultimately we are compelled to recognise that, to describe a contextual group associative pattern, it is necessary to think, not just in terms of absolute difference from other associative patterns, but in terms of the dominant usage of either time or intensity of dyadic interaction. This dominant distribution of a particular interactive or associative mode is echoed precisely in terms of the resource use within such a group pattern.

Individuation

There is one other main factor of group-as-context which has to be considered here, the process of individuation. In a very general sense this is the process by which the individual as a member of a group uses the group as the context within which his growth of consciousness of self is obtained. Thus, although the group is the medium by which change is achieved, the object of change is the individual.

This kind of use of the group as the context of change is frequently found in the use analytical psychologists make of the group system. While it would be true to say that the group itself is not the primary target of their methods, there can be little doubt that some part of the process has a spin-off, perhaps in the area of belonging, and certainly in the area of trust. So the process is in no way a purely catalytic one.

It is interesting to note that the analytical psychologists originally held little brief for the group as an instrument of change precisely for the reason that many operators like it best, that it brings into operation the pressures which enforce conformity. In other words they did not like the pressure which appeared to convert indi-viduals into group members, believing that such pressures would act ultimately to the detriment of individuation by stultifying it with a change of focus.

Continuum pattern

If we pursue the concept of dominant usage mentioned earlier it will be to discover that, whereas the form can exist as an almost pure state, the group-as-instrument is almost always a development out of the contextual form. Moreover a group associative form is discernible in which both instrument and context forms exist at different times in the life of the group. As I have already commented on the fact that the instrumental form has to be created and on the difference of skill and power of the group-centred leader, there is little need to expand upon that theme. However, as the combined form is by far the most common, its nature should be examined.

If we regard any group as an energy system, the input of large amounts of energy from the leader may be expected to coincide with periods when leader dominance would be appropriate. It must remain a purely hypothetical speculation as to the amount and kind of energy which is actually required to maintain a group as a functioning entity, but, for instance, in closed groups it is noticeable that leader energy output is highest at certain crucial points in the group's history: at the beginning, at the end and at crisis points in between.

All systems tend to run down because they consume more energy than they produce, but there is some difference from this sequence of events when the energy cycle in question is that of a social system:

> Social systems however, are not anchored in the same physical constancies as biological organisms and so are capable of an almost indefinite arresting of the entropic process. (Katz and Kahn, 1969, p. 95)

This intrinsic mode of energy cycle may be supplied with external energy by support from the supra-system in which the group is embedded or by pseudo-energy which is derived from the previously uncommitted energy reserves of group members.

Often enough the function of the leader is described as pseudo-extrinsic in that, from his commitment to the group, he will initiate an increased personal energy input and also attempt to inspire and generate an increase in energy input from others. Because group members have not been together long enough to have created a high level of reward satisfaction for themselves, or because some situation has been reached which causes a withdrawal of commitment and energy, some groups cannot at these times and for these reasons produce enough energy intrinsically to reactivate the system. They need to be fed with energy from some external source or from the one person in the group with an ongoing responsibility for its existence – the leader.

This excursion into entropic processes should serve to demonstrate that, as in most groups the energy transformation process is patchy in its effectiveness, it requires support. Inevitably this can produce an associative pattern which is group-oriented, interspersed with bouts of leader-orientation – a pattern which is described by Lang (1972) as 'semi-autonomous'. Although Lang intended this description to define a 'form' of group applicable to particular kinds of client problems and stages of maturity and ability, it also defines the transient stage between group-as-context and group-as-instrument and is also applicable to recurrent patches of a leader-oriented pattern during the life of a group-centred group pattern.

As we hope to show later, these associative patterns have a great deal of influence on the generation of certain obstacles to resource use and on the development of groupwork techniques designed to deal with such obstacles. But first it is essential to consider their relationship to created and adapted group forms. Groups are *created* and *adapted* for groupwork purposes. This bald definition of the areas we must now consider has to be refined in order to present clearly what is meant by created or adapted groups. As the groups we are concerned about are those which form the basic working unit in the practice of groupwork, we should start with a look at groupwork itself before looking at a group form defined by groupwork practitioners and theorists as the 'groupwork group'. Underlying this form is a whole series of assumptions and beliefs which, if they were to lie unexposed, would diminish the accuracy of our understanding of the nature of group. Haskell (1975) called these beliefs the 'Presumptions of Groupwork' and we shall examine them closely. Finally it will become possible to discern the differences between created and adapted groups and more importantly to note their relationship to the associative patterns discussed earlier.

If it were possible for the overworked hypothetical man from Mars to take a fresh view of the people of earth, he would probably be impressed by the amount of time they spend doing things together in groups. (Cartwright and Zander, 1953)

Stressing that man is a social animal has to be balanced by noting the consequences of joining in, or being born into, groups. The security, confirmation and belonging which membership in a group can provide have their counterpoint in the exclusivity that is generated in a group. Simply put, groups exclude as well as include and, as conformity to group norms is a large factor in acceptance by the group, it becomes apparent that the obverse of the enfolding nature of group belonging is the shut-out feeling of those who are not members.

Conflict can thus arise between groups where, because of group conformity pressures, norms have developed and been maintained which are widely at variance between one group and the next although their members may have had common origins. Thus hostility, aggression and prejudice grow and are reinforced. In our search for the reasons why groups work and in any attempt to generate 'artificial' groups for the purposes of benefit to members, it is wise to remember that it is not possible just to select the warm, enfolding factors of naturally occurring groups in creating or adapting a group for groupwork purposes. It may only be possible to alter the balance in favour of one or the other of the major factors. For example, in sports teams the group support system is used to enhance the aggressive competitiveness of the members vis-à-vis other groups in the same area of achievement; in specific problem groups the membership is protected from a destructive sense of difference and isolation.

In the previous chapter it was stated that groupwork was the conscious application of principles derived from the analysis of 'natural' groups with the aim of achieving certain reasonably well defined goals. It now becomes necessary to explore this statement in somewhat greater detail. Bruno (1957) gave as the reason for the development of groupwork the following: 'a social technique is made necessary by the loss of those devices and controls for the realisation of personality that are automatically supplied by the customs of an earlier and more stable society'. While there is some scope for quibbling with this statement historically, in that 'earlier and more stable' societies may well be a myth, there is no quibble with the general idea that change generates instability.

Particularly is this so when much evidence points to a great increase in the speed of change so that, whereas it might once have seemed that ideas and behaviour were handed down little changed from one generation to another, it now seems that few ideas or even social institutions remain the same for very long. Even if institutions do remain the same, the attitudes of people to them change and render them more or less obsolete. Alvin Toffler (1970) suggested, indeed, that stability was a thing of the past and that the future state would be one not only of a ready acceptance of rapid change, of transient relationships, but also one in which advantage could be taken of this state of affairs.

Groupwork, like many other so-called 'caring' techniques, has arisen as a way of helping and supporting, of teaching and of ameliorating the condition of those who, for whatever reasons, find some difficulty in coping both with themselves and with those parts of their society with which they are in immediate contact. It must, therefore, be founded on ethical assumptions about the rights of individuals to develop whatever powers and aptitudes they possess, to be free of persecution, to be able to make choices and adapt to the fundamental necessities of society, to be cherished and to cherish, to protect and be protected. But above all groupwork is based on an assumption that those who need help shall receive it, which must imply at some level the need to intervene in the lives of people on the basis that (a) they may not know how or be able to help themselves, (b) it is necessary to protect them or society or (c) they may not even be aware that they are in a state which requires help. There is a long, compli-cated and ultimately unresolvable philosophical argument to be made here about the ethics of intervention which includes legal definitions (Mental Health Acts and so on), mandates, rights of the individual to live his life in his own way and so on. All have been rehearsed many times and values have been stated and re-stated, but it suffices to say here that groupwork of any kind is interventionist, whether it is mandated by the group members or by society or even when it is termed self-help. What really matters is that, for groupworkers, groupwork is a job; that is, it is actually directed to achieving desired ends; to this it must be added that it is a job for which practitioners, in most cases, will be paid.

Of course groups are used in most forms of human activity, in work, in play, in decision making, in management, in teaching, in learning, in enjoying oneself and in just living. But the word 'use' in this context has enormously varying degrees of intent and equally varying specificity of aim. For our part we are mainly concerned with groups which are 'used' with the specific intent of achieving what have been called groupwork ends, which is to say in general towards enhancing the quality of life of the disadvantaged. In this context it may be useful to look at what a groupwork group might actually look like and in particular at what kind of expectations and values might be supposed to influence it.

The social groupwork group

Rosenthal (1970) claimed to have identified in the groups used by social workers a unique entity within the genus 'group'. Thus:

> it is not only a medium through which individuals can be helped (or through which individuals can be transformed into members), or through which social goals can be obtained, but it also has fundamental significance as a societal building block, or vehicle through which culture is linked with individual character and vice-versa.

This unique form of group may be a conceit but at least it gives a valid basis for examining a little more closely what groupwork groups actually are and whether there is any real justification for such a marked distinguishing definition or whether it should be regarded as an overstatement and that such groups are rather defined by selection and the emphasis placed on particular features which are common to all groups.

To start, then, from Rosenthal, he offered seven distinguishing features of a social groupwork group:

1. it is a unique form of social process which differs from other groups;
2. it emerges from the knowing use by the groupworker of the pre-group processes of acceptance, engagement, organisation and beginning group formation;

3. it is characterised by the involvement of individuals in shared space;
4. it exists in its own collective time;
5. it develops its own inner horizons and an element of consensus about the way things are spoken about for much of the time;
6. it develops an emotional quality with emerging feelings that express vitality and creativity;
7. it changes individuals into members.

My quarrels with this presentation are twofold, but neither criticism is that the statement is untrue. The first is that it is somewhat pretentious and hides very simple and ordinary truths in obscuring language, and the second is that all but the second item are common to most, if not all, forms of group. What we are left with is the simple fact that a social groupwork group possesses whatever distinctive characteristics it displays by virtue of the purposes and values of the groupworker who convenes it and ultimately the purposes, values and intentions of the group-worker's employing agency. This point will be considered in more detail later under a discussion of the presumptions of groupwork, but there are other aspects of the social groupwork group to note first.

Although little appears to have been written about the criteria of selection of the use of groups, what there is should serve to give a clearer idea of what social groupwork groups are by examining what groupwork practitioners and theorists say they are designed to achieve. Lang (1973) analysed a considerable quantity of material written by groupworkers to discover what it revealed of the stated reasons for choosing groups as the unit of service. Her conclusions about that choice can be listed simply as follows:

1. the choice between a one-to-one (dyadic) relationship with its implied intensity or the dilution of that intensity which would be available in a group (polydyadic) relationship;
2. whether group functions and uses were suited to the needs of the potential members;
3. whether a group could be formed into which the potential members could fit effectively;
4. what form the group could take; that is, what were its func-tioning capabilities, how the groupworker would fit into the

conditions of the group and what position such a worker would hold within the group;

5. what kind of influence would be available in the group – basically whether it would be group-centred or worker-centred, or some combination of the two.

It is interesting to note that most of what Lang is saying could be condensed into a statement of the nature of the degree of appropriateness of a proposed group in terms of matching design and available resources to the needs of the potential group members. Statement 5, it will be noted, is a simple presentation of the associative patterns discussed earlier in this chapter.

Northen (1987) indicated that the selection of a group as the preferred unit of service was dependent upon two principal factors: the purposes proposed for such groups by workers and agencies, and the characteristics of the potential members. In the first category she placed (1) the enhancement of social relationships, (2) the enhancement of social competence, (3) the development of capacities to cope with devastating events, and (4) elements not directly concerned with clients, such as staff training and development planning. In the second category were (1) isolated individuals, (2) those threatened by the closeness and dependency of a one-to-one (dyadic) relationship (see item 1 in Lang's list above), (3) those with limited verbal ability, (4) those in need of stimulation and affective responses, and (5) those who are heavily defended. Northen also points to the fact that some writers have suggested that social groupwork may be contra-indicated in the case of those with powerfully rigid belief systems, who are very markedly different from other potential group members and those who show the potential to suffer intense stress from group membership.

Again what emerges rather clearly from this is that social groupwork groups are those groups which are set up or taken over by social groupworkers. The message is not confused. If what Northen and Lang were writing about is what they derived from research into what groupworkers said they were doing and the kind of groups they were operating, then it would only be logical to assert that what was being described were group forms moulded by intentions and by value systems compatible with social work and groupwork principles and suitable to the needs of given clients.

Like most other forms of groupwork which are nominated by their practitioners as specific and different, the specificity, the distinguishing factors, lie almost exclusively in the choice, selection and emphasis of those group elements which are common to all groups. This partisan choice of those elements of group design to be preferred is almost wholly precipitated by the purposes and value systems of the group operatives. Thus psychotherapy groups are simply groups which are shaped by the concepts of psychotherapists and indeed social groupwork groups are groups which ultimately manifest the ideas, aims and values of social groupworkers; self-help groups display in their structure and operation the aims and purposes of their group members, and so on.

This point was most ably illustrated by Haskell (1975) in a powerful article which seems to have had little effect in breaking down what are in essence pseudo-distinctions in groupwork erected and maintained by vested interests. It is very noticeable that analysis is very prevalent at the present time, but synthesis is in no way highly regarded as far as groupwork literature is concerned.

The presumptions of groupwork

No apology is made for borrowing the title of Haskell's paper (1975), for what he has to say in it has a crucial bearing on this stage of the discussion. In essence Haskell's argument was that there was an amazing lack of realisation amongst groupwork writers and practitioners that, as he put it, 'Certain values are implicitly wired into the group program', so much so that what we look at as the processes which occur within groups may not be such universal natural occurrences as we believe, but in some way a projection of the values that we as practitioners 'wire' into the systems we create or adapt.

It is instructive to review briefly the areas that Haskell discusses: the presumptions of lawfulness, of wisdom, of tabula rasa, of democracy and finally of functionalism.

By *lawfulness* Haskell means that there are assumed to be observable and constantly recurring patterns within a group. His conclusion is that 'these ostensible group recurrences, like deductive logical conclusions, are direct consequences of the implicit ideological premises on which a group is postulated'.

The presumption of *group wisdom* states that groups are wiser than anyone or any minority of individuals. However, as Haskell points out, groups are often sensitive to the leader's bias and respond accordingly. Given the pressures which exist in groups, Haskell believes that groups are much more likely to produce what Janis (1972) describes as 'Groupthink, based in a leveling, self-validating group process', the effect of which is to maintain stability and order rather than to produce empirical or rational decisions based upon information.

The assumptions of *tabula rasa* are that (a) the past has no affect upon the group, (b) the past can be trusted, and (c) the group is a tabula rasa, a blank sheet waiting to be written upon.

With *democracy* the basic assumption is that 'countervailing forces will keep power out of the hands of the few'. But, as Haskell points out, the conditions which allow democracy to become operational – (a) a harmony of interests among group members, (b) access to pertinent information, (c) decisions being made within a rational framework, and (d) members having equal influence – seldom seem to exist in groups so that 'democracy' becomes an end in its own right.

In essence the assumption with *functionalism* is that order exists in society because it benefits members of that society; thus there is pressure brought to bear to conform with the existing order.

Given that the arguments presented here have some validity, any observation that is made about social groupwork groups must take into account the value systems of the convenors. Especially is this so as these value systems may be those of a particular, and minor, segment of society rather than those accepted by the majority. The evidence of the influence of value systems is probably irrefutable and, although a powerful factor and one consistently ignored in terms of the offered explanation of observed phenomena, it has to be considered alongside other factors. One of these must be expectations.

All people have expectations of any social situation into which they may enter. The 'fit' of these expectations in relation to the actual situation can range from very poor to very good, depending on circumstances. Like value systems, expectations can most certainly affect group outcomes and they are equally valid in this sense for both group members and group convenors and leaders. Bearing these facts in mind, it will be necessary to treat the observed features reported in groupwork literature with some caution, because even constantly reiterated and repetitive descriptions of processes must be discerned as being contaminated by the values and expectations of those who record them.

So, despite the rash of non-relevant absolute distinctions in groupwork, like the social groupwork group, it is clear that social groupworkers have at least two different starting-points for the implementation of their aims and intents. These are groups which are in existence prior to the groupworker's intervention and groups which are created from separate individuals by the groupworker.

Created groups

The basic fact about 'created' groups is that a new organisation or system is formed where none previously existed. So much of groupwork practice and literature is concerned with the process of bringing into groups people who, it is believed by the convenors, will benefit from this process along the lines indicated earlier. There may well have been some consideration of group membership as a countervailing measure to the alienating and isolating effects of modern society and to the diminishing influence of families as they shrank from extended to primary form. But despite this there has always been the protestation that created groups are not 'natural', in that they are not spontaneous and are therefore in essence 'artificial'.

The main thrust of this argument may stem from the sense that groups created in the hope of enhancing the quality of life of their members pose threats, arising largely from the fact that such artificially created groups are outside the normal run of existence. But this is not so. Artificial or created groups exist all through our society. It is not the act of creation which is regarded as artificial, suspect and threatening, but the purposes for which the act of group creation is intended.

Much of the deliberate intent to generate an influence and energy system, that is a group, to enhance social relationships or social competence or other such intents is thus seen as interference and threat, whereas, if the intent of the groupworker/convenor is expressed as being to develop and use the inherent resources of the group, both individual and collective, this is an aspect of group use which is very readily understood by people who have experienced the need for collective action in teams, gangs, families and work groups all their lives.

The essential basis of a created group lies in the perception by the creator(s) that such a group is not only feasible but advantageous and so we find that there is an abundance of information about planning and preparation and also about the need for a heavy initial input of energy and effort on the part of the convenor. The skills of the groupworker, to be discussed in greater detail later, which are needed at this point are based on an understanding of the kind of needs which can be met in groups, of the ability to organise such a group into being and to hold it until the rewards of membership become apparent. The associative pattern here is often quite markedly leader-oriented, for the very simple reason that at this stage it is the common relationship of all members to the leader which is uppermost and it is the leader's knowledge, foresight and skill in and around the group processes which actually make the group process possible.

Adapted groups

'Adapted' groups are essentially a redefinition or a rejigging of an already existing group unit. It is not necessary to expand greatly upon this particular distinction because it is obvious. The family therapist who takes on a whole family as a group is adapting a pre-existing group to the process of therapy dictated by his values and intents. So, too, is the street worker who works with a gang of adolescents, and so too are a whole variety of other workers who take as their basic unit of service delivery an already existing group, a team, a work group and operate within a set of values and with aims which, if not alien to the group in the sense of being unknown to it, are at least unfamiliar or different.

The planning process here is no less necessary than in created groups, but it is different. The essential structure of the group, its purposes and relationships, its power and communication system are already in place and the concept of artificiality is not usually present. Nevertheless the groupworker, by establishing his own credibility as someone of value to the group, has to use and redirect these existing structures and patterns to serve different ends and possibly to aid this process with the introduction of new ones.

One large obstacle in this process is of course that the membership also exists before the groupworker's entrance to the group and acts as a constraint on what is possible because the process of selection of members to facilitate the groupwork process is not easily available. Adapting groups is often a process of realigning the perceptions of members, whereas created groups have the added facility of being a changed or novel situation for their members. Finally, whereas it is often possible that in a created group which becomes almost wholly instrumental in its associative pattern the groupworker may become a member in the sense that he, like the original members, becomes a known resource but with no more or no less directive input than the rest, this is very seldom an option for the groupworker operating with an adapted group.

The following simple diagram (Table 3.1) shows very baldly the relationships between associative patterns and created and adapted groups, some of which have been already stated. The general tendency is that adapted groups are leader-directed and, though that tendency may diminish as long as the leader remains in contact with the group, he will have to accept some degree of distance and exclusion from it. When such a leader leaves the group then, indeed, the group's associative pattern may well be almost wholly that of group-as-instrument.

Ultimately, whatever form a group may adopt or be influenced into assuming, its main function is the productive and beneficial use of the resources to which it has, or can develop, access. And so

Table 3.1 *Group as context and as instrument*

	Context	*Instrument*
Created group	Leader is convenor; works with individuals	Leader develops group from convened individuals
Adapted group	Leader takes on existing group; works with individuals	Leader facilitates existing group into a large element of self-governance

it is to the nature of those resources that we must give our attention in the next chapter.

Propositions

2. There are two definable forms of groupwork groups: 'created' and 'adapted'.

2a. A group is *created* for groupwork purposes by the coming together of a number of individuals for a shorter or longer period of time, this coming and being together constituting a fundamental and necessary condition for the achievement of their goals and one which occurs under the aegis of a groupwork convenor or convenors.

2b. A group is *adapted* to groupwork purposes when an already existing group, created, formed or arising for purposes other than those of groupwork, is entered by a groupworker or groupworkers with the intent of working with the members of that group to achieve specific groupwork ends.

3. Consciously created or adapted groups may take either of two polar forms defined by the nature of the associative patterns involved: instrumental or contextual.

3a. The *instrumental* associative form of a group occurs when the principal requirement of the group is to have access to and use of the collective resources possessed by and available to its members, known as the 'assembly effect'. (Collins and Guetzkow, 1964, p. 58)

3b. The *contextual* associative form of a group occurs when the principal requirement of the group is for its members as individuals to gain access to and to use a scarce individual resource.

3c. The polar positions of instrumental and contextual associative patterns may lie on a continuum of such patterns.

3d. A group during its existence may exhibit different associative patterns at different times.

3e. Both instrumental and contextual associative forms may be either *created* or *adapted*.

4

Resources

All history – as well as current experience – points to the fact that it is man, not nature, who provides the primary resource, that the key factor of all economic development comes out of the mind of man. Suddenly, there is an outburst of daring, initiative, invention, constructive activity, not in one field alone, but in many fields all at once. No-one may be able to say where it came from in the first place; but we can see how it maintains, and even strengthens itself. (Schumacher, 1974, p. 64)

Resource – something to which one can turn for help or support to achieve one's purpose. Resources – available assets. (*Oxford Paperback Dictionary*)

If a man or a woman possesses the knowledge and skills necessary to repair and maintain a television set and also the opportunity to exercise that knowledge and technical ability, it is not at all difficult to describe such a person as a 'resource' or as possessing 'resources'. There are few who find difficulty in accepting that such a person fits very closely the *Oxford Dictionary* definition of a 'resource' quoted above. The fact that a skilled technician can so obviously do things, understand the workings and thus also the non-working of complex equipment, elicits little wonder – only thankfulness that there are such people who can 'do' things that the rest of us cannot do. Perhaps it would be truer to say that our inability to do such things may be due to the fact that we have never had the interest, inclination or aptitude, or even the oppor-tunity to do them. We may have the potential under different circumstances.

The point is obvious: that some human resources are readily

recognised and acknowledged as such. But, it may be argued, such skills can be taught and learnt; the fact that one person rather than another has such skills may be entirely due to the fact that A considered that the allocation of the time and effort necessary to acquire them was high on his list of priorities, while B either did not consider them at all or had placed them near to the bottom of his list of priorities. This is the concept of choice so beloved of economists as a method of describing the ways in which 'economic' man disposes of his spending money.

The argument becomes infinitely less easily followed when factors which are seldom regarded as resources and which are not so obviously conscious choices and for which teaching and learning situations do not exist in the precise way that they do for television engineers are considered. The 'resources' to which we refer are those which an individual develops which enable him to exist within society; they are the so-called 'coping' skills, the social competencies, the learned behaviour patterns.

Why is it that these 'human' resources which relate closely to 'personality', learned behaviour and endowment and which define, maintain and control the kind, level and effectiveness of each individual's adjustment, should be so little considered positively and indeed should draw down major attention only in their obvious deficit? If, as is postulated here, the almost exclusive reason for using groups and working with groups is to gain access to resources which are greater in extent and different in kind and quality from those possessed by any individual, then we must first look very carefully at the basic material – the resources of the individual.

General ideas on resources

> But as things are, *because our time and our means are limited* and because there are alternate ways in which we can use them, we are continually being faced with economic problems. We are continually considering how to allocate or 'economise' our resources and our time so as to get the most satisfaction from them. (Thomas, 1957, p. 12)

Groups are set up or redefined in order to achieve given objectives. The reason they are set up or so redefined is that there is an assumption, often not made wholly clear, that such a group possesses attributes or assets which will actually facilitate the attainment of those objectives – if this is not true then the exercise would be at best cosmetic and at worst completely pointless.

Individuals possess resources both actual and potential and they have developed resource systems, coping mechanisms, by means of which they apply their assets to deal with the situations met with in everyday life. Both the systems and the resources may be wholly adequate or they may not. They may be adequate some of the time or with some kinds of situation and so on. Collectively the resources and systems of several people should theoretically provide better, more adequate cover than those available to the individual alone. At the very least they should offer the possibility of different choices and the necessary support for trying out some of those choices. But there are problems, not least in the recognition of what we have called 'resources'. Some problems lie in the direction of collecting together into a group those individuals whose apparent assets offer the best possibility of providing resources to deal with difficulties and problems. Other problems exist in the need to create a system from these discrete and disparate individual systems; units which will facilitate the recognition of such resources as do or will exist and the offer of sharing these resources and of developing the ability to use them.

In the groupwork literature and elsewhere the concept of human resources is variously presented as, for example, coping mechanisms, the profile of abilities or as self-awareness and self-actualisation. But there are some distinctions which need to be made. In the first instance there are those genetic endowments and the developmental processes which generate the unique individual. This is where the concept of self-image is attached to the idea of human resources, for it becomes a relatively stable and enduring concept of the individual held by that individual of what he is and of what he is capable. Without doubt this self-concept is usually only partially true in that many possible extensions of existing capability have never been made, some have never been explored and some have probably atrophied from lack of being exercised. Herein lies the potential for change, growth and development which is almost an article of faith for all the so-called 'caring' professions.

But in some way distinct from this, though yet part of it, is the knowledge of what an individual is capable of which has been acquired by actual doing and which becomes accrued experience. This again works in two ways: learning that some things are possible which may have been considered not to be so and, conversely, learning that some things which are thought or believed to be possible are unavailable or unattainable. The first of these categories may be described as a set of habitual response patterns tried and tested – the tramlining effect – as the limerick puts it most succinctly:

> There was a young man who said 'Damn!
> At last I've found out that I am –
> A creature that moves
> In determinate grooves,
> In fact not a bus but a tram.' (Langford Reed, p. 49)

This implies that the actual functioning totality of a person is usually less, sometimes by a considerable amount, than the potential functioning of that person and herein lies the scope for possible change and development so clearly articulated by writers like Maslow, Rogers, Reich, Angyal and others. Shaw (1974), writing about self-structures, says: 'They refer to the fact that, as a result of socialisation, an individual comes to take a partly conscious, partly unconscious view of his own totality.' He goes on to describe 'self-structure' as consisting of 'a set of attitudes towards, or beliefs about, one's own needs, goals, abilities, feelings, values, prejudices, self-characteristics and methods of relating to other people'. He postulates that being mentally adjusted equates with the degree to which these disparate elements are integrated with one another. He also states that the whole structure can and does operate at a number of different levels, for example (1) as a filter of experience, (2) as a framework to lend meaning to experience, and (3) as a guide to the making of decisions and choices and to the selection of possible alternatives.

The self-structure is described as being very difficult to change once it has been formed – hence the suitability of the term 'tramline'. A similar approach can be discovered in the concept of 'coping mechanisms' which is extensively used in Crisis theory. Strickler and Allgeyer (1967) defined coping mechanisms as 'those aspects of ego functioning designed to sustain psychic equilibrium by regulating and controlling the intensity of anxiety-producing perception of real or fantasied external changes that involve loss or threat of loss'. This is the point when awareness of the inadequacies of habitual or usual response patterns is exposed by their inefficacy in dealing with a real or supposed situation. The equilibrium becomes disturbed and the very fact of this disturbance opens up the possibility of change because of the perception of the inadequacy of the self-structure.

It is now necessary to consider certain facts about individual resources in the light of the foregoing. In the first place, because they are developed, discovered and integrated by individuals with a different genetic heritage and different exposure to experience, these resources are significantly unique. This is the factor which makes the combining of differences in a group situation produce a pool of resources not only greater than that possessed by any individual but also of greater variety and character. Choice becomes a relevant opportunity.

We must note that differences are either of degree or of kind, or analog differences and digital differences. Analog differences are differences of magnitude, frequency, distribution pattern, organisation or intensity of a similar factor. Digital differences are those which are concerned with opposites, with distinction and with distinct uniqueness of factors. Lacan, quoted by Wilden (1980, p. 21) says, 'The child's first discovery is that of difference – the difference between self and world.' This difference, once perceived, opens up, when allied to the potential for change noted earlier, the direction and nature of any change which might take place, a salient point when we come to consider groupwork techniques later.

Much human resource potential has been suppressed by the culture in which individuals have matured. Expectations confine response patterns and stultify growth and development in those areas which are considered to be of little value or sometimes to be actually evil or damaging. Potential or possible growth may well then be locked away and barred not just from expression but from development also.

Part of the process of constructing a personal resource system lies in the development of choice. One way in which individuals find their resources inadequate to cope with some situations is that they make inappropriate choices and deploy resources badly and in most ineffective ways. Economists describe such actions as incurring 'opportunity costs', because possible benefits and opportunities have been lost by not using a resource in its best (best for the individual, that is) alternative way. Differences between individuals, when revealed and accepted, would tend to show some of the possible alternative choices, which might have constituted a better point of application of the resource. This points once again to one of the major reasons for group use.

Thus the ideas of personal growth are consistent with the concepts of resource discovery, resource development and use. Given that 'spare capacity' exists, learning about it makes it available for use. It may not be used, but at least it is known about. Extra assets have been discovered. But there are, as ever, problems. In order to gain access to hidden or unused assets, even to change the existing use of known and habitual response patterns involves an element of risk. The equilibrium of the individual which is the self-structure can absorb the impact of small external forces and remain stable by making readjustments, which implies a temporary imbalance and then a return to a previously existing state. But where large forces or even unknown forces exist (in the sense of those which have not been met previously) the inability to readjust by a process of integration creates an unstable, non-coping state. Thus, even though change can only be brought about by the development of a new state of equilibrium, the process tends to be resisted because of a perception of the existence of threat – loss of stability and security and the diversion of essential energy. This particular manifestation of resistance will be dealt with more fully when we consider it as one of the more powerful obstacles to the use of individual resources and to the process of these being shared.

Other problems concerning individual resources are very simply stated and indeed have already been implied. The first concerns recognition. If a group of ordinary individuals is asked, 'What resources do you know you possess?', it immediately becomes apparent that most people do not consider what they do or the attributes they possess in this kind of way. Indeed resources are often only accepted as being present when they have already been demanded by the needs of a particular situation and produced or found wanting.

Again many people, while quite aware of their competence in

many aspects of their lives, have no great esteem for what they can do. They tend to believe that what they can do everyone else can do as well and, usually, that most other people are more able than them. Thus individual resources are often masked by a marked lack of self-esteem, probably promoted by the inadequate development of coping methods and by the inappropriate use of those which have been employed. A marked lack of success soon clamps a very firm constraint on the size and quality of the self-structure components.

It is therefore essential to realise that the resources which form the basis for the development, enhancement and change of an individual's responses to his existence are there, but may be restricted by many factors, and that they require a conscious effort to generate recognition of their existence and even more effort to make them visible and available in the face of perceived threat and of the effect of stability-maintenance factors. Ultimately the un-freezing of these assets also implies that a certain openness has been created which offers the possibility that resources, in the form of awareness of alternatives, may be taken and used. But this involves different acts of willingness and, as we shall see, different aspects of trust. Increasing a willingness to give does not auto-matically generate a willingness to accept, or, having accepted, a willingness to use what has been received. Having briefly discussed the essential and fundamental material of groupwork, individual resources, we must now turn our attention to the processes of collective resource use and the concept of sharing. In its essential detail a group is a unit, a collection of individuals who learn to pool some of the resources to which they as individuals have access and where these pooling and sharing activities become mutually beneficial and life-enhancing.

Collective resource systems

There are large individual differences among people, both in ability and personality. Human motivation is complex and no one ever acts as he does for any single reason, but in general, positive incentives are more effective than threats or punish-ments. Conflict is no more inevitable than disease and can be resolved or, still better, prevented. Time and resources for solving social problems are strictly limited. When something goes wrong, how a person perceives the situation is more important to him than the 'true facts', and he cannot reason about the situation until his irrational feelings have been toned down. Social problems are solved by correcting causes, not symptoms, and this can be done more effectively in groups than individually. (Miller, 1969, paraphrasing J. A. Varela)

An assembly effect occurs when the group is able to achieve collectively something which could not have been achieved by any member working alone or by any combination of individual efforts. (Collins and Guetzkow, 1964, p. 58)

The ideas of sharing and pooling which occur when considering the collective resource system which is a group need some very careful scrutiny. What actually occurs to create the 'assembly effect' described by Collins and Guetzkow is rather complex.

In the first instance, as individuals feel that they have something to contribute to a group, that contribution, whatever its form, has to be made visible, known and thus available, to the other members of the group. That much is universal. But what comes next is dependent both upon the nature of the contribution which is being offered and upon the needs of the group at that particular time. For instance, the collective and shared nature of individual resources may be cumulative. The actual force, physical or emotional, which may be required in a group to move something could be well beyond what any individual member has the ability to apply. But if several members join together, the cumulative exertion of force at the point of need can achieve the necessary motion with relative ease. This is a simple case of more of the same which adds up to what is required. The essential process is one which takes a common asset and, by providing an understanding of the kind of need which exists, generates a willingness on the part of group members to supply that asset in a co-operative and cumulative manner. This cumulative process often becomes the basis of a support system where individual members find themselves encapsulated in warmth and understanding.

As we have suggested, resources are individually possessed; the process of exposing them makes them available to others, so a second collective usage must take the form of difference, both analog and digital. For example, a group of individuals with a common problem will, by reason of their diversity, have sought and found ways of coping which, in the very differences of approach, reflect that diversity. If it now becomes possible for those different approaches to be revealed, what must become almost immediately apparent is that each individual has by no means tried all the approaches on display.

Thus the immediate collective advantage is to increase the area of possible choice. This simple statement, true though it is, in no way contains all the possible advantages. There is the distinct possibility that becoming aware of different approaches (different in the sense of their being not previously thought of ways, as well as containing differences of emphasis and intensity of ways already thought of and tried) has a catalyst effect. In essence this produces a response to the perception of difference which triggers a new and spontaneous idea or set of ideas which may be additional to the triggering idea or may be wholly different. The advantage of increased choice covers ideas, responses and behaviour patterns; it demonstrates the possibility that situations and problems and methods of coping are frequently far more diverse than any one individual is able to appreciate without help. We are all in the situation of accepting that the resources we use frequently constitute the totality of the resources that we possess. But what is worse, we may believe that they are also the sum total of resources available anywhere. This occurs despite abundant evidence that circumstances frequently cause individuals and groups to reveal that they possess capabilities over and above what they would normally have accepted as possible. Indeed the repertoire of resources which most people will admit to possessing is one which has been defined over time and made visible by being called into existence by circumstances.

What I have called collective resources is a phenomenon which is based upon the recognition of difference. Such recognition is not likely to occur in the individual in isolation, or much more likely to occur in the individual when confined to familiar circumstances. A person entering a group of strangers is not wholly aware of the differences which may exist between himself and the other members until such differences are exposed. Indeed, as all studies of the entry of newcomers to groups have firmly established, the security needs of such entrants tend to dictate that they will seek as many and as relevant similarities between themselves and others as they can.

Even when the group-in-context is the form in use and the major resource may be the group leader, whose knowledge and skill, more directly applied through a relationship based in credibility than the resources which will ultimately become available in the group-as-instrument, it is the resources of the group members which pick up and use direct information and provide support in the process. In the extreme case where individual growth, change, development or transformation is the end to be achieved, it is still the resources of the group as a whole which make this possible by being the reflector of behaviour and by forming a mini-society in which the social experimentation around more adaptive behaviour patterns can be essayed in comparative safety.

Having stressed the nature of the difference of resources which collective exposure can generate, it is also necessary to say something about similarity. As has been indicated earlier, one of the commonest forms of group is that which is created around the perception of its members or of its convenor that a common problem exists. It is often stated in groupwork literature that this commonality produces a bond that is based on the diminution of the sense of isolation and of idiosyncratic peculiarity that people attempting to cope with problems frequently feel is their lot. Without doubt such a relief does occur, though it is seldom strong enough in its own right to overcome the perception of difference which also occurs, usually before these differences have been demonstrated as possible assets. Thus differences, particularly those which appear to confer advantage, may start with a negative connotation. The problem which this can create is well known amongst people who work with groups as that of holding together group members with a common problem but of great personal diversity long enough for that diversity to become an available asset in terms of increased choice rather than a source of discomfort.

Collective resource has still another facet, that of complementarity. In economic terms this is called division of labour and may well be one of the most powerful factors in the success of the group-as-instrument.

The group will have access to more extensive resources than an individual member. Depending on the nature of the task and the effectiveness of the group's interpersonal relations, these extra resources will either inhibit productivity or be utilized to produce an assembly effect bonus. The most crucial feature of the task is the extent to which it lends itself to a division of labor. A task so structured that divisions of labor are impossible makes it difficult for the group to utilize its potentially greater resources. (Collins and Guetzkow, 1964, p. 52)

Indeed the concentration upon the roles which obtain in groups is indicative of this aspect of complementarity. Some commentators go so far as to say that, when a group is deficient in some of the task roles which are essential to the achievement by the group of its avowed and espoused aims, selected members with the capacity to learn should be coached in the necessary role functions. Napier and Gershenfeld (1973), skating, as they admitted, on 'very thin ice' when referring to the ideal working group, put forward as one of the criteria of success that:

Roles in the group are varied and differentiated according to both interest and performance. In other words there is a concerted attempt to discover appropriate resources, depending upon the particular need at a given time.

After the cumulative resource situation perhaps complementary resource use is the next longest in existence. Its basic premise is quite simply that there are many situations in which human beings find themselves where the resources of an individual are deficient in some important respects. There are three possible responses to that situation: (1) the individual can make do with his deficient resources and endure the consequences, or (2) he must seek to acquire personally the resources which are required, or (3) he must seek the resources of others to supply or augment his own deficiencies. The second and third of these options are both situations which could be coped with in the confines of a group and indeed they are both frequently dealt with at the same time in the same group.

In the next chapter we will be concerned to discover those factors which make the discovery and use of resources difficult to achieve, so it is only necessary here to mention the problem of recognition. When a group of people is asked directly what resources it possesses the result is usually confusion, plus many requests for a clear definition of what is meant by resources. However if a problem is posed to the same group and they are then asked what resources they have available to cope with it the answers are significantly different. In the second instance the group are very likely to request time to discover what resources exist within the group, that is given that they do not already know, by asking direct questions related to what they perceive as need. Thus we can have a very clear perception that human resources can be most readily defined in direct relation to the known need for them.

For instance, if a group within an organisation wishes to influence the decision-making procedures of the organisation in specific areas and in specific directions, what is needed becomes reasonably obvious. It is related to the collection and presentation of information of exactly the kind that the organisation uses to base its decisions upon. Now the group may well possess an abundance of such information, but, as often happens, they may have no real knowledge of how to feed it into the system in such a way that it cannot readily be ignored. Once this situation is appreciated (and sometimes this can take quite a long time, because the group may well believe that the value of their information is self-evident) then the needs become much clearer. The group can then look for resources which can at least go some way to meeting their needs.

It has been my experience that resources within the group's reach have often been around for a long time, resources which could be applied to the particular problem in hand, but they have not been used because there has been an absence of recognition of their relationship to the problem. For this reason material on decision making and on problem solving always makes clarification of the problem an absolute priority. The very act of clarifying the problem or the matter to be decided upon tends to define the resources necessary to meet the situation.

Of course this is an oversimplification. Many other factors affect decision making and problem solving which have little to do with the situation itself but a great deal to do with the motivation, aspirations and attitudes of those involved in the problem-solving and decision-making processes. So, while it is not true to say that clarity and understanding of the needs will elicit appropriate responses and ensure successful outcomes, it is absolutely true to say that the successful application of resources to any situation cannot occur without clarification.

This leaves us with a familiar problem of recognition which is that of similarity of patterns. Over the years an individual becomes able to recognise the pattern of certain situations and he is aware of the resources he has deployed in the past to cope with them. Thus each individual has a repertoire of resource response patterns. If they are not used frequently some reminder may be required. So when members of a group are relatively familiar with one another it becomes possible for one member to stimulate another by drawing attention to the fact that the current situation bears some resemblance to some past event and to elicit the resources which were used then.

With many people who seek help or support or growth in groups the recognition of assets has a degree of incredulity about it: if they had assets they would not be seeking help. Of course this is untrue. Resources have not only to exist but, as the groups seeking to present information in their organisation frequently discover, they need to be used in an appropriate manner, in the right place, at the right time. There are so many places where the process is open to fault, deviation or inappropriate application that, although resource discovery and use are unquestionably the basis of all forms of groupwork, effective use is quite a complex and formidable task.

Propositions

4. The factor of value in human groups lies in the individual and collective resources possessed by and available to the gestalt of group members and leader.
4a. The principal generative factor of that value is the creation of the perception of 'difference in similarity' or 'complementarity'.
4b. This principle is most active in the instrumental associative group form.
4c. Another generative factor of that value is the creation of the perception of resources of special quality.
4d. This factor is most evident in the contextual associative group form.
4e. Both generative factors can occur in both group forms.
4f. The resources of individual human beings comprise the

totality of their experiences, knowledge, skills, understanding, abilities, insights, imagination and feelings.

4g. Human resource may be actual, that is known and available, or potential (forgotten or not previously exercised) but probably susceptible to being developed.

5

Obstacles

> The basic question to be answered in the study of group problem solving is: How best can a group use the resources of its members in solving a given problem? This phrasing of the question assumes that the necessary resources do lie in the group. (Hoffman, 1965, p. 99)

Clearly Richard Hoffman is concerned to discover two factors. The first is that the problem facing the group is one which is within the capacity of the group to solve, a point which will be of great importance later when we consider that one of the major obstacles a group might face is the fact that its abilities and the problem it faces are in no way commensurate. The second point that Hoffman stresses is that the resources should lie within the group, and it is here, it is suggested, that his statement is too restrictive.

As we have seen in the previous chapter, the resources which are available to a group are not only the immediately accessible nor even the potential ones, but also those resources which exist outside the group but to which the group members have access. The two-way influence across group boundaries which is usually described as 'the seepage effect' is also an apt description of the way resources behave. No group member is free of the effects of life outside the group, either positively or negatively; no life outside the group for group members is wholly free from the effects which arise within the confines of the group – again either positively or negatively.

The use of the term 'obstacle' to refer to any let or hindrance in the group situation to the discovery and use of resources is relatively uncommon, but arises directly out of the need to consider resources as the prime reason for the existence of all groups. When the resources under consideration are human resources, those factors which inhibit their employment are also largely human. Hoffman, indeed, uses the term 'inhibit' in his exploration of what might impede group problem solving. But he also goes a step further:

> Even if the group members have the capability of solving the problems assigned to them, other questions remain. What factors tend to prevent the effective utilization of the group resources and what factors promote problem-solving efficiency? (Hoffman, 1965, p. 100)

Although we are looking at a wider remit for a group than that of problem solving, it is such a major group activity that it is instructive to look at in some detail.

The first step is to agree with Hoffman that to discover what he calls the 'inhibiting factors' is only part of the process. Even if it is possible to remove, diminish or circumnavigate these inhibiting factors, Hoffman states that this alone is insufficient to secure effective problem solving. He then postulates that it is necessary also to apply 'facilitating factors'. This two-pronged attack on obstacles will indeed be followed here, in that in this chapter we shall concentrate on what constitutes inhibiting factors, while in Chapter 6 we shall look at methods not just of removing, diminishing or circumnavigating them but also at the facilitative techniques which are available.

The process of discovering what resources are available to a group which has been created or adapted with particular goals in mind must be concerned very largely with the ability of group members to explore their resource repertoires and with the sense that freedom exists to express ideas and feelings within the group. Nearly all groups, when discussing their immediate concerns, tend to generate a pressure towards agreement. In simple terms members who are concerned that their group will stay in existence, presumably because it provides some satisfaction for them unavailable elsewhere, will tend to move towards a consensus in order to remove the possibility of disintegrative conflict. Thus, as in all human interaction, an element of control is exercised over what is contributed. In itself this maintenance gambit may be necessary, but it also has an inhibiting effect on the production of ideas, thoughts and feelings which are perceived as 'different' or risky. An obstacle to the free circulation of ideas has thus arisen out of a perfectly natural care and caution about the continued existence of the group.

This movement towards consensus is related to perceptions of risk, threat, security and trust and thus inevitably also to the factor of time. It is axiomatic that group members have to convince themselves of the consequences of risk taking and without question this is only truly achieved when those consequences have been demonstrated within the normal procedures of the group. These demonstrations are a function of time spent within the group.

Once more it is essential to show that behaviours designed to meet a given set of circumstances can often develop into obstacles to resource use. Thus 'Processes which were initiated by people to ensure safety threaten to become the very traps which make work in group impossible' (Goldbart and Cooper, 1976, p. 255). Ford, Nemiroff and Pasmore (1977) discovered that there was a great degree of confusion amongst researchers concerning the degree to which established groups developed a tradition, an accepted pattern of dealing with their problems which did not exist in 'ad hoc' groups. What they found was that, where a group utilised a consensual approach to decision making, it required much more time to complete a task than did conventional interactive groups. The extended element of time may well have been concerned with the suppression of difference mentioned above, especially as Bass and Dunteman (1963) demonstrated that unanimity, that is consensus procedure, had little bearing on the effectiveness of task performance. Indeed it was suggested that the more complex the group task the more detrimental in arriving at an effective solution the promotion of consensus appears to be.

Glover and Chambers (1978) discovered that 'as structure is increased in small groups, three of the four components of creativity, fluency flexibility and originality decrease', thus backing up Hoffman's contention that conditions which prevent the free expression of ideas are the main barriers to the effective use of group resources. Amongst the factors of group structure that Hoffman lists in this situation are:

1. Group size: unless group members have a great urgency and need to contribute, the larger the group the more inhibiting

its size becomes for members who have strong introvertive tendencies and a fear that dissent will be equated with deviance;

2. formal structure: this diminishes the 'railroading' effect powerful speakers may have, but, as just noted, it also tends to reduce the creative production of group members by enhancing security measures;

3. power structures: the ideas of high-status members receive greater attention than those of low-status members and certainly the perception that power resides in certain individuals decreases the creative input of low-status members; also, as communications within groups tend to be addressed more to high-status members than to low-status members, the former have the ability to monitor and select which contributions are to be accepted by the group and to what extent.

When examining predictors of group performance Melnick and Rose (1979), suggested that a group needs some members who are high risk takers. They perform the 'break in' function which is so necessary to begin to loosen the binding effect of 'tramlining'. Of course if the risks taken form a quantum leap for most members then they may have the opposite effect on low risk takers by increasing the sense of fear and threat based upon a perception of an inability to operate at the demonstrated level. Melnick and Rose also indicate that it is necessary for low risk takers in a group to be helped to develop an expectation of support and closeness as quickly as possible to prevent drop-out in the face of what may be perceived as a situation of unacceptably high demand. Hoffman (1965) also lists as possible obstacles to group performance the personal characteristics of members:

1. lack of confidence in own judgement;
2. attempts to obtain popularity by agreeing with other members;
3. having a strong need of the group, producing uncritical agreement with group norms;
4. insecurity generated by possible rejection;
5. conformity to avoid accusation of deviance;
6. conformity to the openness of liked members and those seen as capable;

7. inflexibility of approach based upon the success of previous approaches;
8. withdrawal upon rejection of initial ideas;
9. those who talk most tend to have undue influence on group performance.

Apart from the consideration of obstacles to decision making and problem solving in groups, evidence of hindrance is to be found in the material on defence reduction, trust formation, self-disclosure, choice dilemma and risk taking and on group performance in general.

Discussing the unresolved feelings of fear and distrust with which members arrive in a group situation, Jack R. Gibb (1964) wrote that the symptoms of distrust included:

> persistent defense of one's public image, attempts to change attitudes and beliefs of others, attempts to make decisions for others, avoidance of feeling, avoidance of conflict, advice-giving, flattery, cynicism about the powers of the group, derogation of the group's abilities, maintenance of formality in behavior and in control mechanisms, lack of confidence in the product of the group and denial of membership.

The development of trust within a group is consonant with the development of perceptions of the consequences of risk taking. Often an increase in self-disclosure is regarded as stemming from a concomitant increase in trust. Group members have watched how situations involving some risk and disclosure have been handled and have built up a repertoire of expected responses. If these predictable response patterns are such that they satisfy the need for safety then defence reduction can take place. But the two absolutely necessary elements to the development and production of this state are time and direct observation of the appropriate response patterns.

Thus ultimately distrust, one of the main obstacles to the accession to group resources and thus a major factor in the quality of group performance, can only be reduced by the individual member becoming aware through observation of the predictability of certain kinds of risk taking. In this there is involved the element of choice. It is possible that members may well see how to bring about a desirable outcome for the group but at the same time be aware that in the present state of their understanding the cost of procuring such an outcome may be unacceptable. Thus the choice may well be to refrain from committing themselves and their resources to the achievement of such an outcome. The perceived cost of any social action has to fall within acceptable limits before such an action will be entered into. The cost may be estimated against both short- and long-term rewards, against both open and hidden gains, and all of these may be intensely individually assessed. But until the cost/reward ratios have been tangibly and visibly established the ignorance of consequence is one of the major obstacles to efficient group performance.

Davis (1969), listing the variables which affected group performance, what he called the 'resistant phenomena', included the following:

1. group size;
2. group composition: (a) intellective abilities and performance, (b) personality traits of group members;
2. group cohesiveness: (a) the effects of cohesiveness on performance, (b) the effects of performance on cohesiveness, (c) co-operation and competition;
4. norms.

In essence Davis is articulating what is becoming abundantly clear, which is that many factors which have a positive effect upon a group's performance may also, under appropriate circumstances, prove to be amongst the group's most determined obstacles. This leads to our need to consider in Chapter 6 the idea of 'appropriate consequence', in which it will be necessary not just to recognise what is actually happening but also whether the consequences of what is happening will turn out to be obstacles, a hindrance, rather than an enhancement of resource use within the group.

In a chapter on obstacles to effective interpersonal relations in a group, Collins and Guetzkow (1964) noted the following:

1. individualistic motivation – self-oriented behaviour;
2. conflicting patterns of interpersonal relations traits: (a) different patterns of interpersonal relations orientation,

(b) differences in amounts of prejudice, (c) different patterns of managerial traits;
3. status incongruity;
4. homogeneous or heterogeneous personalities and backgrounds.

Much of this is echoed by researchers into other group forms.

T Groups were basically concerned with the process of learning and so whatever constituted an obstacle to the learning situation was of interest. As there is a large element of learning in all groupwork it is instructive to look at what Benne, Bradford and Lippitt (1964) considered to be obstacles to that process. They offered the following list of barriers to learning which, as we have just noted, as learning is the prime process in T Groups, is in essence a list of obstacles to the effective functioning of the group:

1. seeking easy, early answers;
2. conflicts between the familiar and the unfamiliar;
3. resistance to the breakdown or compartmentalisation of the individual;
4. reluctance to expose thoughts and behaviour to others;
5. defensive reaction resulting from lack of individual security;
6. lack of skill in assessing behaviour;
7. lack of conceptual structures to plan the direction of change;
8. hesitation to accept or to give helpful reactions;
9. lack of connection seen between laboratory and potential utilisation.

Once more there is a remarkable similarity between the obstacles in even so specific a group approach as the T Group and the findings of other groupworkers. If we substitute the word 'group' for 'laboratory' in statement 9 above there is a clear reiteration of the commonest causes of lack of commitment to a group – the perception that what is happening in the group has little or no relevance to everyday reality and the problems thereof.

In her chapter on research in T Groups, Dorothy Stock (1964) commented on several patterns of behaviour which occurred with sufficient frequency to acquire the label 'syndrome' and which could be classed as 'obstacle' behaviours. One was the 'stepchild' syndrome, where the individual group member's main worry was about the way he was treated by the others and whether such treatment could be changed. Another was labelled 'the innocent bystander' syndrome, whose concern was self-oriented security, in that all problems within the group were seen as belonging to someone else. This constituted a withdrawal from the group usually characterised by the withdrawer 'becoming an observer'. These obstacles arise mainly because, for whatever reason, members retreat from or do not offer a commitment to the group, which effectively isolates them from use of the group's resources or from contributing much to the resource pool.

In the literature of social groupwork there is but little consideration of those factors which either promote or constrain a group. This may have arisen from the attitudes of the writers which tend to be constrained within an ambit constructed round the concepts of providing a professional service to a client population. However there are some pointers which contribute to the discussion presented here.

As in any problem-centred enterprise – casework, research, education, psychotherapy – obstacles to the pursuit of the group's basic work will require diverting energy to the task of finding ways through and around them. (Schwartz, 1971, p. 9)

Schwartz implies that the removal of obstacles, those impediments to the working of the group, is a primary group objective and one which needs the application of effort. Attention to the processes within the group is not, he says, an end in itself but rather it is the means by which obstacles may be overcome.

It is my contention here that recognising, diminishing and/or disposing of such obstacles, as they are the main impediment to gaining access to group resources, is the primary aim of all groupwork. So it is necessary to scrutinise what constitutes such obstacles and to show (as is attempted in Chapter 6) how that understanding can give rise to the techniques for dealing with them.

First it is necessary to highlight an important change in what have become the standard approaches to groupwork. It is significant that, in all the groupwork literature to which the author has had access over the years, very few writers have discussed or even mentioned the idea of obstacles to resources or affirmed that the practice of groupwork is specifically an interactive methodology for dealing with them. The reasons for this are to be found in the attitudes that groupwork writers have to the practice of groupwork which, stated baldly, are that it is a professional service which is supplied to clients. Despite all the ideas put forward about being non-judgemental and democratic, the underlying trend in practice is still one of 'giving'. The attitude change to which reference is made above is one which admits of the professional skills of the groupworker but defines them as creative; that is, skills in the creation of a system which generates the possibility of the resources within that system, and known to it, becoming available. Thus, as we shall see later, the techniques of groupwork lie in the field of creating opportunity. This is in no way to decry the service-giving aspect of groupwork but rather to remove it from its central position.

In one sense obstacles to the production and use of resources within the group can be seen as stemming from sheer unfamiliarity with the ideas and methods and aims of the group, or even lack of awareness:

> The existence of these obstacles is usually obscure to the group member himself. His awareness is limited by his incomplete vision of the common ground and by his own defenses, to distinguish between internal and external deterrents, and to assess his own productivity at any given moment. (Schwartz, 1971, p. 21)

But indeed a swift cull of groupwork literature begins to yield a list of possible obstacles which is almost infinite. In order to give a clear indication of what might be regarded as obstacles much material has been condensed into three major areas: (1) general constraints, (2) personal characteristics, and (3) perceptions related to being a member of a group. These are presented in chart from (Table 5.1) for easy reference and then discussed.

It is of course impossible to list all those factors which might at some time or other constitute obstacles to the revelation and use of resources within the group. Indeed even those elements which are apparently good, in that they can help the group to achieve its objectives, are, in certain circumstances, to be classified as obstacles. For instance, the ability to verbalise ideas, thoughts and so on, which is a highly prized asset, can become an obstacle when its use blocks the production of ideas and thoughts by the less verbally facile group members.

Thus the purpose of Table 5.1 is to indicate those main areas in which obstacles can and do arise, with some examples of each. For when we come to consider the techniques of groupwork it is necessary to show that the recognition of the nature of obstacles to the production and use of group resources is the essential basis of the development of means to remove or bypass such obstacles.

Table 5.1   *Obstacles to resource access and use*

General constraints	*Environment:* organisation, accessibility, ethos, association; material resources; time; group size; management, etc.
Personal characteristics	*Lack* of understanding of what is required; of value to others; of different ways of doing things; of drive; of esteem and of knowledge
	Belief that certain things are impossible
	Habits of caution, hiding, mistrust, suspicion, resistance, doubt, inferiority, isolation, rigidity, avoidance, ignorance and 'tramlining'
	Attitudes of self-blaming, of strong need to be accepted; authoritarian
	Experience of low tolerance of ambiguity, self-centrism; of restricting reference group; of wrong knowledge; of tradition, rumour and hearsay
	Skill: social incompetence; low level of participation and of communication, specific training
	Status: low, powerless
	Relationships: inability to make and maintain
	Needs: survival; identity, power/control; acceptance
Perceptions related to being a member of a group	Unfamiliarity, ignorance, anxiety, lack of information, of perception, of utility; ambiguity; need to withdraw, fear of being submerged, imposed upon, rejected or of being diminished; similarity to previous bad experience; threat of change, of being exposed, of pressure and influence and of unreasonable demands; disagreement about group procedure; lack of credibility of group and/or group leader

General constraints

Environment.   The first and most obvious effect brought about by the environment within which a group operates must be physical – the dimensions of the room, the furniture, the lighting, the use by other groups and for other purposes which leaves evidence of such occupation. Multiple occupancy reduces the sense of privacy; evidence of particular use as, for instance, a classroom is often associated with memories which may or may not be conducive to easy acceptance of the venue as one appropriate for current group use by some of the members.

There is some evidence that people have expectations of venues in the same way that they have expectations of institutions and people, based on the nature and quality of the information they already possess, whatever the accuracy or actual quality of that information might be. It is also fairly obvious that people adjust their behaviour patterns to conform to what they believe to be appropriate to the environment in which they find themselves. Where that behaviour is in some degree of conflict with the aims and purposes of a group being held in that environment, a constraint which is in effect an obstacle is in operation.

Perhaps the major factor in this form of obstacle formation is that the restraint, the caution which the environment inspires, is rarely considered as the cause of behaviour patterns. In the words of Schwartz, quoted earlier, the cause is 'usually obscure'. This leads almost directly to the process of incorrect ascription. Because the real cause is either unknown, unthought of or obscure some other explanation is necessarily offered for the behaviour pattern. In this case the most likely offering from observers is that it springs from sources to be located in the personality of the actor. From the actor's point of view, the explanation of the behaviour tends to lie, though often somewhat vaguely, in a direct response to the situation in which he is enmeshed. This phenomenon has been carefully explored by Jones and Nisbett (1971) in their paper on the divergent perceptions of the causes of behaviour. The process was also noted by Rosenberg (1956).

Material resources.   The constraints exercised by material matters is most obvious in the terms of finance, appropriate utensils, equipment, furnishings and so on. Indeed so much is this the case that groupwork texts are clear about the need to revise what is possible in a group situation if the necessary equipment is not available.

Time.   As this is a factor which will occur repeatedly within this text it is appropriate to make only a brief comment here. It is obvious that time has been used in the formation of all the problems to deal with which groups are formed. It is therefore axiomatic that time will be required for these problems to be dealt with. What is much less sure is that the requisite amount of time will be available, either because there is a lack of the necessary skill to estimate how much should be required, or more likely because the organisation in which the groupworker is employed cannot give the time required, either through lack of the necessary knowledge or through sheer inadequacy of the time available to meet all the tasks with which it is faced. But if the correct amount of time is not devoted to the process of group formation and work then this in itself will constantly present as an underlying obstacle and impede progress, not necessarily entirely, but in a multitude of insidious ways usually expressed in some form of need for safety or caution.

Group size.   Most of the disadvantages of group size are to be noted in the section below on perceptions of being a member of a group and lie in the swamping factor of sheer size. But there is also the problem that large groups can and do allow people to hide and thus, whatever contribution they might have been able to offer, if given the chance, does not emerge because they have to all intents and purposes been 'lost'.

Management.   The constraints here lie along the lines of the provision of inappropriate structures in which groups cannot function effectively or in expectations which are not consonant with the time and resources available.

Personal characteristics

[It] seems clear, as common sense will suggest, that member characteristics such as intelligence, aptitudes, and specific abilities have a direct and positive impact on performance. (McGrath and Altman, 1966, p. 55)

McGrath and Altman, in their generalisations from small group research, describe what happens in groups in terms of 'performance' both of individual members and of the group as a unit. By implication that performance is actually the visible manifestation of the impact of obstacles and constraints operating in the group situation, but they also write, 'it may not be possible to predict the performance of a group as a group, from the knowledge of individual abilities however measured'. The difference between the assessed capabilities of members and their performance in the group can only be the product of obstacles which inhere in membership of the group, or more accurately in the perceptions of the members of that group. This particular point will be dealt with in the next section.

Amongst those personal characteristics of group members which have been noted as influencing group behaviour in what might be called an obstructive way are attitudes, status, experience, intelligence, skill (abilities) and expectations, all of which we will discuss in time. But it must be realised that the influence of member characteristics on group performance is neither a direct positive nor a direct negative one. It is much more likely that this cause/effect relationship varies. To quote McGrath and Altman once more, 'we may be in a realm where either *too much* or *too little* of a characteristic interferes with performance, with some optimum, in-between point enhancing performance'. Thus the techniques of groupwork aimed at removing, diminishing or circumnavigating obstacles to resource use is not and cannot be a straight response, but has to be a duly considered one, bearing in mind the appropriateness of what is occurring. For example, the domination of a group by one member exercising one of his personal characteristics is wholly inappropriate in most aspects of groupwork and must therefore be considered an obstacle to the use and development of group resources. However, in a time of some dire emergency, when support direction and leadership may be at a premium, it could be a wholly desirable characteristic and thus a resource rather than an obstacle.

Perceptions related to being a member of a group

When people form a group, for whatever reason, the sense of strangeness of the members is one of the major obstacles to their becoming able to integrate, to accept what Collins and Guetzkow

(1964) refer to as a perception of having a 'common fate'. If all the members of a group are starting at one and the same time, their past experience of similar situations, combined with their personal characteristics, will dictate the response patterns they will emit. Classically people wait until they have some clearer idea of what to expect, and of what is expected, before they begin to resolve how much or how little of a commitment they are prepared to make to this new venture.

One of the reasons why groupwork literaure is so replete with material concerning the admission of a newcomer to an established group is that the situation throws into stark relief the problem – of overcoming the caution, the suspicion; of the need to gain access to the new resource and not frightening it away. The problem is one of how to establish the rewards for co-operation and commitment. Perhaps one of the major factors involved revolves round the degree of need for affiliation that new members have. If it is great, then it may be powerful enough to minimise the strangeness and the need for caution.

Deutsch (1958) indicated that, besides co-operation, there were two other basic forms of response to becoming a member of a group – the individualistic and the competitive. Of these the individualistic approach is the more interesting in that it is in essence a natural response based on self-preservation. Bass and Dunteman (1963), in their Orientation Inventory, included a self-orientation scale which at a high level of self-orientation, that is, one which is self-protective and individualistic, produced the following description: disagreeable, dogmatic, aggressive–competitive, sensitive–effeminate, introvertive, suspicious, jealous, tense–excitable, manifestly anxious, lacking in control, immature–unstable, needing aggression, needing hetero-sexuality, lacking in need for change, fearing failure and feeling insecure'. Obviously this list of self-oriented behaviours could equally well have been included under the heading of personal characteristics, but, in that it describes behaviour which is essentially a reaction to the presence of others, in precise terms to being a member of a group, it is perhaps more appropriately offered here.

The list of perceptions related to being a member of a group offered in Table 5.1 are nearly all aspects of resistance to the process of affiliation, a denial of, or at least a caution about, the tendency to join or to be with others. Man is a social animal, but the question has always been not one of whether or not to join but how much to offer, when, and how much to retain. Brehm (1966) coined the term 'reactance', defined as the resistance to group influence. He asserted that reactance was generated in a group member by a feeling that his freedom (status as a free agent) had been threatened. It is essential to point out here that Brehm's reactance lies between what might be considered a necessary caution and scepticism in the face of new ideas and new situations and a stubborn refusal to countenance anything even slightly different from 'usual'. Even reactance can become a habit and an end in itself, a stand taken for its own intrinsic merit against all forms of change. Opposition to authority is often necessary for maintaining a balance and in countering its over-zealous use, but it can become a crusade in its own right, without any logical justification.

In 1956, Rosenberg postulated that groups provided the basis for what was called 'evaluation apprehension', literally performing functions and tasks under the scrutiny and observation of others, causing the arousal of anxiety and frequently resulting in a diminished performance. Thus fear that the observer will diminish and devaluate the actor is a very prevalent one and, indeed, a constant cause of the undervaluation of competence. Of course the nature of the observer and the relationship perceived to exist between actor and observer may be crucial in the degree of apprehension engendered. In fact one of the greatest strengths of a group, that its individual members are aware of each other's presence, is something of a two-edged sword. Until some ability to predict, based upon experience of a particular group, is available, the presence of others, especially others who may be seen as powerful, knowledgeable and expert, is often a great obstacle. This is especially so when personal characteristics of shyness, lack of self-esteem and lack of socially competent behaviour patterns exist in group members. Then the defences against involvement, such as opting for the role of observer, come into play which can ultimately lead, if they are not dealt with, into a withdrawal from the group if this is possible.

It is necessary to realise that many people find themselves in group situations by no choice of their own. They are directed into them either compulsorily or because their circumstances indicate that some form of group care may be necessary. Without doubt this enforced and patently unwilling membership forms an enormous obstacle to the use of individual and group resources, sometimes even being so powerful as to cause the withdrawal of resources previously readily available.

An enormously powerful obstacle exists in the withdrawal of commitment, which may indeed mean withdrawal from the group. Many groupworkers have complained of the disastrous effect of psychological withdrawal and of apathy where the scarce resources of the group are drained by the employment of the energy required to carry one or more non-contributing passengers. In this brief coverage of the reactions to membership as obstacles to resource use it remains only to look at one or two further examples. The presence of others, as in a group situation, can frequently cause distraction and embarrassment to the extent of promoting an increase in blunders and other incorrect and inappropriate responses, if not completely inhibiting any response pattern at all. Again the actual cohesive quality of a group may well enfold a new group member and engender such satisfaction from a purely social involvement that it produces a group norm of non-productive behaviour lest task-oriented behaviour detract from the socialising.

Finally there are the perceptions related to threat. Fundamentally these are founded on the ambiguity of the member's needing the group and yet having a very real fear of what the group may demand of him. These expectancy effects, if in balance, produce a situation of apparent immobility which has the overall outcome of denying access to resources in either direction.

It should be clear from the foregoing that obstacles to the pursuit and use of resources produced by constraints, personal characteristics and perceptions of the group situation itself are multitudinous and naturally derived from learned social behaviour patterns. It must also be stated that, although these obstacles are very obvious in the beginning stages of a group and during the admission of a newcomer, they recur at all stages during the life of a group as experience within it produces an effect upon the individual member's expectations and perceptions. The whole process of a group becoming self-directing, for instance, is based upon a learning programme for the members which changes their perceptions and expectations of the group to the extent that they become able to use their knowledge and understanding, gained by being in and of the group for a period of time, to gain access to and use the existing resources: 'The greater potential resources of a collection of individuals mean that a group is more likely to discover an alternative than a single individual' (Collins and Guetzkow, 1964, p. 52).

Proposition

5. The basis of all groupwork is to create or adapt human groups in either contextual or instrumental form or in some combination of both to generate actual and/or potential resource systems to meet the actual and/or assessed needs of group members and to *remove, diminish, change or circumnavigate obstacles to the discovery, recognition, accessibility and use of these resources.*

6

The Techniques that Groupworkers Use

> It is possible to perform acts that are techniques without employing groupwork, as well as to use these same techniques and be doing groupwork. The techniques are not unique to our field; they are shared by all of the helping professions. (Klein, 1972, p. 147)

There is a danger, as Klein points out later in the same chapter, that semantic confusion can arise over the differential use of words like 'technique' and 'method'. Klein's argument was that method was put into practice by the use of techniques which in themselves were not the sole possession of groupworkers. However, such is the degree of caution, that groupwork literature is full of the stated aims of groupwork which are clearly and explicitly noted, but when the question of how these aims are to be addressed, when some executive process is looked for, the available help, if any, is given in the most global terminology possible.

Of course this caution is based upon the need to prevent the idea that groupwork is a 'bag of tricks' which, once learnt from some handbook of techniques, is all that is required. Indeed such handbooks, lists of games, activities, progammes and so on actually exist. For instance, Bertcher (1979, p. 7) writes:

> And in every one of these groups there are some basic techniques which, if used correctly, can help to make the group successful: successful as regards both goal achievement and participants' satisfaction.

It is interesting that Bertcher could list the following as techniques: (1) attending, (2) seeking and giving information, (3) contract negotiation, (4) rewarding, (5) responding to feelings, (6) focusing, (7) summarizing, (8) gatekeeping, (9) confrontation, (10) modelling, (11) mediating, and (12) starting. There is a marked similarity here to the lists of leadership roles and to the Bales (1950) Interaction Profile, which, while it is not surprising, is indicative of the wide range of terminology which may be used to describe what are essentially identical situations.

Toren (1972) noted that, if groupwork was essentially therapeutic in orientation, the techniques used would be those of psychotherapy in general:

- encouraging the expression of feelings;
- bringing to the surface and discussing anxieties and fears;
- generating more self-awareness and new insights into problems and more rational coping methods.

In Toren's opinion this is done through transference, countertransference, intra-psychic conflict, resistance, interpretation and insight, 'whereas social groupwork promotes democratic attitudes and behavior patterns. The groupworker may function as a teacher of skills, a leader of program, a mediator, an advisor, a limiter, and a friendly counselor' (Scheidlinger, 1953).

While counselling programmes teach the broad basis of the aims of counselling, they also contrive to inculcate specific techniques to bring about those aims. The fact that such precision is significantly lacking in groupwork instruction must imply a considerable difference in the quality and probably in the complexity of the aims involved. This is a crucial point. To state it a different way, the aims of groupwork have been so obscure in their complexity that no simple statement of the means of achieving them has been possible. However, if it becomes possible to say that all groups, of whatever form, focus or setting, have some degree or aspect of a common aim, it then becomes relatively simple to present the techniques for achieving that aim.

It is maintained here that the aim common to all groups, of whatever focus or form, in whatever setting and based upon whatever theoretical concepts, is to discover, release and use the resources available to the group. This being so, those factors which prevent or discourage the achievement of this aim – the obstacles – are, of necessity, the prime focus of attention. So it becomes possible to say that the techniques of all groupwork are those behaviours which are used directly or indirectly to effect the removal, diminution or bypassing of these obstacles. Thus obstacles lead directly to techniques for their removal, but of course the obstacles to be removed are not necessarily the same in all circumstances.

When a group therapist works with a group his purpose is to bring about some goal of treatment, such as relief, new insight or enhanced ability to cope. But what that group therapist _does_ in order to achieve that purpose is to generate the possibility that the group, leader and all, can discover and use the resources which are available to it. When a teacher sets out to increase the knowledge of a class in a particular subject area, exactly the same _doing_ takes place. The major resource may be the knowledge possessed by the teacher, but, unless those to be taught can be induced to bring their resources of interest, integration and understanding to bear, the task will not be accomplished. Thus all groupwork is just what the word appears to define: it is work performed by a group. The distribution of resources within the group may be very uneven, but the contribution to the group of what is available should ideally be universal.

So when we talk about the techniques and methods of group-work we are in fact discussing the instruments, the tools which practitioners use as parts of the action they take, which, very basically, is to expose, develop and use the cumulative resources available in the group. This implies not just using the resources which are readily available but also promoting the production and use of other resources by the removal and/or diminution of obstacles which prevent their emergence.

> I find it useful to regard groupwork skill mainly as a response to what is happening in the group. . . The worker's functions are to facilitate and mobilise group process and to contribute to it in useful ways. (Heap, 1985, pp. 58–9)

Heap goes on to say that this conception of groupwork is based on two prior assumptions, the ability to observe group processes and to be able to understand them as well as it is possible to do.

In Chapter 1 Table 1.1 indicated that the material in rows 1, 2, 3 and 5 fed into 4, which was the 'action' column – what group-workers actually do. This matter of techniques, which looms so large in the minds of groupworkers and is so little addressed directly in the literature except as lists of gambits or systems of categories, is one to which we must now give some careful thought. Thus it is proposed to discuss what groupworkers do under five sequential headings – (1) planning, (2) starting, (3) working with, (4) terminating or transforming, (5) assessing and developing – and to show that, in effect, every single action has as its ultimate goal, no matter how indirectly approached, that of gaining access to and using the human resources available in the gestalt of group and leader and containing systems. As has been said above, this process amounts to the recognition and removal, or diminution, of obstacles.

Planning

Planning 'suggests that this is a logical sequence of steps and decisions which can be taken by the groupworker in the planning stages of running a group to most nearly secure the conditions for effective leadership' (Hodge, 1977, p. 8). It is essential to realise that the preparation or planning stage in groupwork, if it is at all possible, is extremely important, in that the quality and the efficiency of such preparation makes a strongly marked impression, not just upon the early days of a group, but upon its entire existence. It is almost beyond question that neglect at this stage produces effects which are difficult, if not impossible, to rectify at a later stage.

Because preparation is the stage which precedes the actual coming together of a group, the principal resource is the group leader. There are, however, situations in which almost the whole process of preparation is carried out by the prospective group – beyond the initial idea, that is. An excellent example of this kind of group planning procedure is to be found in a paper by Mullender and Ward (1989) entitled 'Preparing for and Initiating a Self-directed Group'.

What is at stake in the planning stage is an understanding of what issues the proposed group will be expected to address; the kind of resources which might be available or developed to deal with these issues; the obstacles which can be reasonably expected to exist or develop, including the constraints of situation; and ultimately what kind of approach and techniques in the light of current knowledge might best be employed. In essence what is being planned for is a functional system which, in the light of the data available, will be the one best calculated to deal with the issues which have been isolated.

The nature of this kind of planning will be more fully explained in Chapters 8 and 9 and in relation to specifically oriented group objectives. Suffice it to say here that planning is largely a matter of scanning the information available and consulting and beginning to make decisions. The first and most important data which must be scanned are those which relate to the needs of the individuals which have promoted the idea that a group may be an effective way of dealing with the issues related to those needs. Much depends here upon the quality of the available data, with regard to two aspects: the nature of the needs and the groupworker's understanding of how groups can operate to meet them. Based upon these two factors (particularly the second), the groupworker should be able to make some basic calculations about the mechanics of the proposed group, such as the number of members; the qualities of potential members, which may be either positively or negatively or neutrally rated in view of the tentative purpose of the proposed group; frequency and duration of meetings; life span of the group; principal activities and its closed or open nature; and finally the probable leadership approaches.

This list must serve to highlight the point that, whatever the ultimate resources a group may work with, the primary resource, which actually exists before the group comes into being, must be the groupworker. Much attention is given in groupwork texts to the processes involved in running a group, even to the form of words which might be used, but that given to planning is often inadequate and limited to factors such as selection. The whole purpose of creating or adapting a group is to build a system which possesses and can learn to use a wider range of resources for coping with common issues than have been available to the individual members in their pre-group state. So it is crucially important, if an enormous amount of energy and goodwill are not to be expended upon maintaining, repairing or changing a deficient and dysfunctionining system, that the initial structure is founded on the best level afforded by the knowledge and skill available.

Needs assessment. Garvin (1981) wrote that potential group member needs fell into four categories, which he defined as anomie reduction, role attainment, social control, and alternative role attainment. Heap (1985) produced the following six categories of aims for groupwork which are essentially the mirror image of member needs: alleviating isolation, promoting social learning and maturation, preparing for an approaching crisis or other life change, solving or clarifying problems at the personal/familial level, solving or clarifying problems in the members' environment and achieving insight.

These needs and aims are very similar to the categories given by Northen (1987), quoted in Chapter 3. Of course there is a problem here, which is that these lists of categories of need have always been compiled by groupworkers and even, in some instances, have been based not so much upon the problems or needs of actual people but upon an assessment of what general categories of need might best be dealt with in a group context. This can still be a useful exercise, however, for indeed there are categories of human problems which have been shown to be non-susceptible to group approaches.

Starting

I think that it is appropriate to reiterate here what seems so obvious as not really to require thinking about: that assessment of need in the initial stages of planning and of setting up a group can only be as good as the information which is available about the potential group members. This is why the whole pre-group process is at best tentative and why the beginning stages of a group, what Schwartz (1971) calls the 'tuning-in period', are crucially important. For it is here that the group and the groupworker begin to make additions and modifications to and subtractions from the knowledge and information base, both in terms of needs and of resources:

The process of preparation, described here as the 'tuning-in' period, is one in which the worker readies himself to receive cues that are minimal, subtle, devious, and hard to detect except by a very sensitive and discerning instrument. (Schwartz, 1971, p. 13)

Thus the recommended technique in the period of starting is one of a conscious heightening of awareness and sensitivity so that the information base upon which the group was originally convened can be upgraded in its accuracy and depth.

Another factor has to be considered here – that of rectifying a common error in groupwork thinking, which is that because groups are a natural and ubiquitous part of human existence the ability to utilise group processes is, as it were, a natural skill. Once this fallacy has been exposed, one of the more obvious techniques in the starting period of a group's existence is the need to prepare potential members for the experience of their membership and to begin the process of learning how to use the system which is in the process of being created. Few people would be satisfied to be presented with a complex piece of equipment with the instruction to work out for themselves what it was and how it should be operated. Handbooks and instruction manuals are a common feature of such equipment, yet we have the unrealistic expectation that without instruction or a written guide human beings can 'work' a group.

Recently Manor (1988) presented a framework for the task of preparing the client for social groupwork in which the main issue was the difficulty of translating information into action, in this case information about what can happen in a group.

Very rarely will the process resemble a straight line beginning with 'selling' and ending with 'buying' a group. Rather, a relationship needs to develop between the worker and each prospective member whereby 'personal' needs are elevated to 'social' goals through trust and explicit communication. (Manor, 1988, p. 102)

The problem is one of understanding. I must admit that in this situation I have always tried to envisage what a groupworker would need to say to me to convince me at least to try a group. Not that this gives any indication of what I might use to convince others, but it does serve to remind me that the motivation and reasons for joining a group have to make a great deal of sense in the prospective member's world as well as in mine, and that these two worlds are, by all significant measures, different.

This is why, whether it is a matter of a personal interview with a prospective group member or the activities of a 'pre-entrance' group, it is essential that much thought be given to the process of 'selling'. It can quite quickly become a process of persuasion or coercion which requires some very certain ethical standards to be acceptable, rather than a process of making effective links with a prior state of knowledge.

The whole process of resource mobilisation and use starts at this point, though essentially the major resource being brought to bear is that of the worker. The groupwork literature has presented many ways of expressing this situation, from concepts of energy input to ideas of direction and control, but, in most cases in which groups are to be systems of value to their members, time and skill, patience and effort are required to bring about the construction of a group from a number of separate individuals. The house has to be built before it can be lived in, even though the building process may be taking place around the potential residents who are also the builders.

Working with

> [Therapy is achieved] by one human being with specialized knowledge, training and a way of working to establish a genuinely meaningful, democratic, and collaborative relationship with another person or persons in order to put his special knowledge and skills at the second person's (or group's) disposal for such use as he/they choose to make of it. (Lerner, 1972, p. 11)

The special skills and knowledge referred to by Lerner in this quotation, when specifically applied in the group situation, are those related to the group, its creation and use. For the group members to make 'such use as they choose' of such a group must imply that they actually have some knowledge of how to operate the group, whether as context or as instrument. In short a very important element of the special skill and knowledge referred to consists of demonstrating what is available, that is the resources and how to use them.

It is appropriate to restate here that groupwork is concerned with locating and using available and potential resources. This being so, the practice of groupwork must be seen to fall into two categories of groupworker behaviour, each significantly different but each with exactly the same aim, which is to bring into being and maintain a system which will provide the necessary resources to cope with certain defined issues. The primary category of group-worker action has been covered in the previous sections of this chapter and relates precisely to the actions of conception, planning and starting, all factors which are to a large extent leader-centred and dependent upon initiative and recognition of needs and on concepts of particular group forms. This is different from what follows, not only in being so leader-centred, but also in existing before the group was an actual entity. The obstacles which exist in this category of worker action are, as we have seen, related to the quality and quantity of information, the practicality of what is proposed in terms of the known constraints and supports and the ability of the worker both to synthesise and to analyse and ultimately to conceptualise from what he knows about all the factors involved the basic and starting form of the proposed group.

However trite it may seem to say this, the next stage is one which can be simply stated as a process of holding. Simply stated, a group can only be said to exist when its constituent parts, its members and leaders, actually stay together. Unless holding takes place a group has no chance to operate qua group because it ceases to exist in any meaningful form. This is not to deny that the tenuous and very brief existence of some groups may be all that is required for a successful outcome in rather special circumstances.

Schwartz (1971) proposed five major tasks for the groupworker:

(a) finding, through negotiation, the common ground between the requirements of the group members and those of the systems they need to negotiate;

(b) detecting and challenging the obstacles to work as these obstacles arise;

(c) contributing ideas, facts, and values from his own perspective when he thinks that such data may be useful to the members in dealing with the problems under consideration;

(d) lending his own vision and projecting his own feelings about the struggles in which they are engaged; and

(e) defining the requirements and limits of the situation in which the client–worker system is set. (p. 16)

But precise as Schwartz's proposals may be, he has omitted the crucial necessity of holding. His groupworker tasks appear to start with a group already in existence. So the first major obstacle which generates the need for the first major techniques is that of the forces and inclinations which push potential members away from belonging, the centrifugal forces of individualism, of security needs and so on.

In very simple terms holding is the transition stage between the conception and the actual appearance of a group. It is a period of fairly intense energy input by the leaders and it depends crucially for its success on generating the belief that the proposed group is a venture worth committing some energy to, a matter which also relates very strongly to the intensity of need on the part of potential members and to the level of credibility of the workers and/or the organisation for which they work. Thus all techniques in this category of worker activity are concerned with providing reasons both rational and emotional for the potential members at least to commit themselves to continuing to attend.

In this exercise several factors are of prime importance to the workers. Of these perhaps the most important is that the groupworker shall have not only some clear idea of the needs of the assembled potential members, but also an even clearer idea of what the group, when constituted, will be able to achieve. It is also necessary to be able to express these ideas in terms which are not only understandable to the prospective members, but actually mean something in terms of their own personal experience. It is well if, at this difficult stage, workers have in their grasp previous related experience, either first-hand or from recorded sources, and can give estimates of the time and effort involved and of the outcomes possible, plus some indication of the kind of procedural structure which can form the basis of starting. But there must also be a clear realisation that this state of contract-like negotiation is only viable at the level of knowledge which is available. Most importantly this implies renegotiation at later stages when new or different information is available.

Other factors which may be exploited are those of curiosity on the part of potential members and the pressure they experience from several sources in order to bring about some change in their circumstances. Indeed the basis of most of the techniques of holding are concerned with time and processes which expose members to the possibility of beginning to learn for themselves what is available. As all educationists are aware, there is a great deal of difference between information which has to be taken on trust from another and information which is derived from personal experience.

Of course there are many groups where this holding and developing process is either not necessary or not possible. In these cases the rule of adaptability is applicable. This states that, where circumstances exist which are not alterable and which diminish or change the desired outcome, the group design must be adapted to achieve the best possible outcome in the circumstances. In extreme cases this may mean that the project has to be abandoned rather than being allowed to proceed, with, probably, very negative effects. The time factor is otherwise crucial. When group members know from their own experience of being in a particular group how things are managed, how responses occur, a knowledge they can only acquire over time and through being involved, they have a credible personal basis for decisions they may make about commitment or withdrawal which are consonant with the thesis of a cost/reward balance.

If holding is successful and even during the process of establishing the group in stable form, other techniques of working with the group become possible, based on the known obstacles to resource access and use.

General constraints. The general constraints shown in Table 5.1 are environmental factors (organisation, accessibility, ethos, association) and material resources (time, group size, management). The probable constraining or supportive nature of the environment in which the group is to be created should have been part of the considerations of the earlier stages, but inevitably the effect that certain kinds of environment can exercise may not be clear until it is actually appreciated by members of the group. Ideas and feelings associated with given environments are frequently dormant, so all that can be done is to be aware of what signals are being sent and to weigh the consequences of both positive and negative responses to them.

There are no simple rules here, merely what Heap (1985), quoted earlier, called a 'response to what is happening'. For instance, in two roughly similar mother and child groups, both inadequately housed, both being compelled by circumstances to have the group for the mothers and a play group in the same room, reactions were very different. One group thrived on the basis of exploring the way mothers responded to the behaviour of their children; the other deteriorated rapidly until separate accommodation for the children could be found.

In most of this area of activity the principal technique is based upon responding with caution to what is actually happening and on making a calculation of the consequences for the resource system which is being constructed of intervening or not and on deciding the form and style of the intervention if it is deemed necessary. But there must also be the continuing assessment of consequence. If constraints compel modifications of the original designed intent, to what extent is it still viable? In other words, will the resource system which it is now possible to create be adequate to deal with the original issues, or is there a pressing need to redefine them?

If it is possible to regard acquiring skill as the development of techniques, a most important acquisition for every groupworker is a personal knowledge of time. One of the basic questions which seldom receive a satisfactory answer is of the order of 'Given the people, issues, constraints, knowledge and skill involved in this group, how long is it going to take to start showing results?' We believe that one of the crucial behaviours in obtaining a high credibility rating amongst group members for a group leader is not only to have some concept of time but to be proved to be accurate or at least reasonably so. Without doubt this particular skill can only grow from experience, but its beginnings can be established by consultation with experienced colleagues and appropriate adjustments can be made for different circumstances.

Group size is another factor which is often determined by circumstances rather than by choice, but here again a groupworker should have a basic understanding, not just of the probable effects, good and bad, of different sizes of groups, but also of the way in which size may affect the precise form and performance of the kind of group it is proposed to run. If size is a matter of choice, that number of members must be chosen which most clearly enhances the development of a group with the resources and access to them which is appropriate for the group's purpose. This implies, as ever, that the groupworker should have some knowledge of the probable effects of given numbers in known circumstances, at least to some general degree.

The last of the general constraints noted in Table 5.1 is that of management. Basically management is the art of providing adequate structures within which the business of an organisation can proceed with maximum efficiency. But this definition implies a state of knowledge on the part of management which comprehends very clearly the nature of human resources as well as their place, utility and fit in the overall organisation. It is in the quality of this knowledge that groupworkers often find a significant constraint which usually comprises an almost total lack of understanding of the way groups work or of what they can achieve, or at best consists of expectations which are not consistent with reality.

Thus the techniques which are of paramount importance in this area are those concerned with the effective dispersal of data in appropriately acceptable form to those who have the power to make decisions about what groups within the ambit of an organisation may be expected to do. This is often a very tricky point because experience shows that management and groupworkers seldom see the same things as priorities. But as those same groupworkers pay great attention to understanding the needs and methods of expression of their group members, so it is necessary to understand the needs and thought processes of management.

Terminating or transforming

The techniques involved at the ending of a group have a significantly different orientation to those discussed earlier. Groupwork writers indicate that the process of termination is the reverse of that of starting and in some simplistic sense this is true, especially if starting is seen as a process of engaging disparate individuals into a group system. But if our concentration is not so much on the process of engagement but on the resources to which such a process gives access, then termination is not just a reversal, a disengagement, but a rather different process. It must be made clear that termination has a variety of forms which are dependent upon several factors. For instance some groups are ongoing – members come and go but the group as an entity has a steady existence. This condition occurs in both major forms of group. What is terminated here is the membership of individuals, the group continues to exist in much the same form and may do so for a considerable period of time.

Where a group has an ordained life time, whether it is open or closed in form, then obviously the whole process can be defined in terms of the group completing its allotted tasks, and when its usefulness is completed it ends. But this kind of theoretical simplicity is often complicated by reality. Thus a group may find that its allotted tasks are not achievable, sometimes because they were established without adequate knowledge of what was possible, sometimes because the resources and commitment of members and leaders is not up to achieving them, sometimes because constraints are changed by events beyond the control of the group.

But if the main reason for the existence of any group is to discover and exploit the resources it possesses or can engender to solve problems, to provide learning, insight, pleasure, treatment, etc., then, however, a group or a member is 'terminated' the central issues are clear. Fundamentally they consist of the pursuance of several processes of which the foremost must be to ensure that the experience of being in the group and whatever benefit was derived from it should be integrated into the individual member's life. This implies that whatever learning about the use of resources which the group has demonstrated should have been absorbed and become available for the individual to use – specifically in the area of recognition of resources and of the obstacles to their use and of the ways in which these latter may be overcome.

Of course, catastrophic changes can occur which makes termination sudden and probably harmful. But even in such circumstances some time, however small that might be, must be used to consolidate and prepare for what comes next. The essence of dependence in groups occurs when resources are used for the benefit of the members, but those members do not either understand the nature of the exact process of resource-use nor do they have the facility to practice it for themselves. In such circumstances it may be necessary to establish some other form of support system for group members who have lost their group membership before the purposes for which the group was established have been achieved.

When a group discovers that either it has completed its original task and in the process has discovered other areas of need or problems which require to be dealt with and are susceptible of such attention, or the group has discovered that its usual form and processes are inadequate to deal with the original issues, then transformation becomes an option. There are two main forms. The first occurs when the group retains its original membership but redefines its aims, processes, rules, etc., to meet the newly exposed issues. The second occurs when the group realises that as constituted it cannot deal with the discovered problems and therefore its restructuring, while keeping sufficient of the original elements, members, etc., to provide for some carry-over, has to take in new members, new and different leaders and design new aims and procedures.

In a very simple sense transformation exists whenever a long-term group decides to use its discovered capacities to deal with an issue different from that with which it has been previously occupied. What happens then is that the group, having discovered during its existence a degree of compatibility and the availability of resources and assets within itself, realises that these factors can be applied with varying degrees of success to issues other than those for which they were originally developed.

Essentially, termination and transformation are groupwork techniques which are wholly dependent for their success upon what a group has achieved in its life span. Members are often reported in the literature as going through a process of grieving when they have left a group based on the fact that they suffer from a considerable sense of loss. Whereas some sense of loss, particularly if the group has had support as its fundamental aim, is inevitable, termination should be illuminated ideally by a realisation of the gains in development, of enhanced insight and of discovered potential. Ultimately the development and utilisation of resources which takes place within a successful group should generate in individual members an understanding of the processes of discovery and utilisation of resources rather than creating a dependence upon the resources themselves. It is the process which can continue to exist and be used when the group has long gone which is the principle aim.

Assessing and developing

Most groupworkers learn a process of assessing what is happening in a group and of developing the resources available to meet the issues which are involved. Indeed, assessment is a process which is never absent from the role of the groupworker and is only efficiently performed when backed by an adequate system of recording which puts events in the life of the group into perspective and into chronological sequence. Much has been written about this practice and it is not the purpose here to elaborate upon it, merely to say that assessment in another form needs a little consideration.

One of the major forms of obstacle that a groupworker may face is that of inadequate understanding of his/her own performance in the resource development process. Group leaders *are* a major resource in all groups whether leader-oriented or not and it is thus essential that the nature of this resource should be understood and the possible consequences of its use even more so. For this purpose assessment is necessary. Feedback from as many sources as are available is the mainspring of insight creation and ultimately of development. It is of paramount importance that group success should be as rigorously analysed in terms of its causation in the same way as group failure often is. It cannot be stressed too vehemently or too often that the groupworker's role is a dual one: namely, that of *being* a resource and one which is conscious of its assets; and that of the *creator* of situations in which others can develop their resources.

7

Resource Theory

Because a practice theory is basically a theory which is created in consideration of its practical consequences it is therefore by definition pragmatic. The tenets of this philosophy incline us to recognise that thought is always in transit and that the processes being described are thus never-ending. Perhaps to say that they are open-ended would be better. Decisions about action have to be taken in the light of the knowledge and information available at the time of making the decision. Then, when the action decided upon is taken, it immediately changes the state of knowledge upon which the action was founded.

One of the major reasons for practice theories being so thin on the ground is simply that, if they are to be true to their subject area, they have to be dynamic rather than static and to generate dynamic concepts in a written, static and linear form implies a whole series of linguistic difficulties. Thus, although it is possible to describe a process such as discovering what resources are available to meet the needs of a given group of people, it must be obvious that the actual 'doing' of this kind of action is an intensely personal process taking place in an idiosyncratic context.

The best that can be achieved under these conditions is to provide some indication of what might be expected and the possible consequences of doing certain things. Above all the legacy of the pragmatic nature of such a theory must be the development of an understanding of the 'freefall' situations which are generated by the very process of taking action. Thought is continually 'in transit' and it is in this respect that the element of risk in action lies.

However, we clearly cannot be satisfied with the mere eliciting of pattern, even if we go about the process systematically and discover a good deal more regularity than has been observed in the past. For a number of very obvious reasons we must go behind the manifest phenomena to see whether *some model of the generating process* can be set up. Not until we have a *satisfactory model* can we be said to *understand* the process fully or to *retain control* over it in *changing circumstances.* (Kendall, 1961, p. 13)

Toren (1972, p. 23) said ' "practice theory" in social work has been developed mainly in a trial and error manner'. She went on to add that it had not developed through research guided by a body of theory and thus had borrowed the theories and findings of the social sciences. This of course engendered an uneasy fit between the production of knowledge for its own sake and the practitioner's concern with the pragmatic business of the value of knowledge in solving problems, in essence its applicability and its effectiveness.

Thus a 'practice theory' of groupwork must be a structure which goes beyond the discovery of what Kendall calls 'regularities' to the creation of a model which, while using those regularities as its base, discovers and exposes some process which lies behind or underneath them all and from which they appear to derive. It must also have the essences of applicability and efficiency described by Toren.

The first six chapters of this book have presented in broad terms some of the borrowings, some of the 'regularities', the ideas, experiences and practice of groupwork. This chapter will endeavour to show just such a process as Kendall describes which fits around all the deviating and divisive paths which groupwork has explored. Chapters 8 and 9 will show that this process or source can be seen to be applicable to some of the existing major groupwork forms and thus, by implication and extrapolation, to all other forms as well. Ultimately such a source must also have implications for the way groupwork is taught and practised and these matters are discussed in the final chapter.

The primary purpose of groupwork

Coffey (1952) defined two approaches to groupwork which he called the 'psyche group process' and the 'socio group process'.

The former was seen as being instrumental in satisfying the emotional needs of its members, while the latter was task- or goal-oriented. He went on to say that he thought these two approaches were not truly different but rather separate ends of a continuum of group process. This is an interesting statement, in that it embodies a position that many writers eventually accept – that all the many supposedly different approaches of groupwork actually stand in some discernible relationship to one another. In Coffey's case the relationship was that of continuum, positions on a straight line. In the case of other writers the relationship is spatial, like the facets of a diamond, or multidimensional. But the salient fact which emerges is that when the purpose of groupwork is being discussed there is usually some perception that, at a different level from that being used in the discussion, the apparently disparate factors are indeed related.

It is the essence of the resource theory of groupwork that at that deeper level of discussion all groupwork is concerned with the discovery, recognition and use of human resources and it is a methodology for removing or diminishing the obstacles which stand in the way of this purpose. In this sense resource theory has a simple relationship to all forms of groupwork practice. It is the one thing that they all have in common.

> In this survey of indicators of group as a preferable form for service, it seems evident that while assorted practitioners have highlighted one facet or another none has yet found a way of formulating an *interactional framework* for assessing appropriateness of group form for service; that is, one which would allow one to view together such components as the nature of the client, the nature of the problem, the nature of the client's particular circumstances, the nature of the group form, the nature of the social work purpose, anticipated forms of influence, and outcome desired. (Lang, 1978, p. 253)

Lang is accepting that groupwork is, or may be, a way of delivering a service to clients in need, but she is also attempting to discover, first, what kinds of need might be most appropriately met by groupwork and, second, what form of group is applicable when the desirability of groupwork has been established.

In essence Lang believes that groupwork, as a form of service, has been around long enough for there to be sufficient material to analyse degrees of appropriateness in its delivery. But more importantly she points to the development of a practice ideology in a piecemeal fashion with individual practitioners 'highlighting' what seems to them important and with scant reference one to another. This is in no way to diminish the contributions of individual workers but is merely to point out that, while such a process may be essential in the early stages of the development of a complex human skill, the time has long passed when it was entirely adequate.

The fundamental question to ask must be: 'What exactly do groupworkers do and what do their groups seek to achieve?' This may well be followed up by a consideration of the fact that, even if groups are used in such a wide variety of ways with apparently extremely different aims in view, the simple fact is that they all have in common that they are *groups*, that is collections of human beings with some continuity of existence and some sense of belonging or membership. Logically, therefore, it would seem reasonable to postulate that the system of association known as a *group* actually possesses, or is able to develop, certain characteristics which are then available for use in a variety of human situations.

What we have attempted to show is that human beings are indeed creatures born and bred to group behaviour patterns and have a strong and basic need for the presence of others, either in reality or, if that is not available, in fantasy. It is also demonstrable that this need can be developed into the use and acceptance of groups which have no apparent spontaneity of generation. This causes problems in the sense that the perception of artificiality in such groups frequently hinders the development of an understanding that, whether a group has the nature of a family and is therefore, by common consent, a 'natural' group or is a group which is consciously and deliberately brought into existence to perform a specific function unattainable by isolated individuals, logically it is still a system of human beings in close proximity to each other over a period of time. Indeed the similarity of all groups is a much more striking fact than the differences of the manners in which they arise or of the uses to which they may be put. This being so, it would appear sensible to search for what all groups may have in common rather than to divide them into species, not just according to natural or artificial origins, but also according to the many and varied uses to which they may be directed.

The most obvious thing about a group, of course, is that it contains a number of people. Given that the effect of a group is to bind people for a period of time to a common cause, albeit often only as a very small part of their overall living pattern, then for all tasks where number and diversity are a basic requirement a group has the advantage over the individual. Without question, if the group cannot bind its members to the common purpose then it may well dissipate the very advantage it was constructed to produce. But herein lies another essential fact. All human beings, as has been repeatedly stated, have developed and grown through a process of group security and exposure. However much this effective conditioning has been suppressed or superseded as a matter of habit or of conscious choice in favour of independence and individualisation, it must still exist. When need becomes paramount, that basic pattern of being part of a group, that essential fear of being compelled to recognise the fact of individual isolation, can be a great motivator to participate in group activity. Thus the first point of any groupwork practice theory must be to realise that, where a task, however defined, either cannot be performed by an individual or can be better performed by several, the necessary scenario for group use has been set.

Groups are clearly defined as containing a number of people, but that is not at all the same thing as saying that many tasks can only be well done by a number of people combining into a group. A group – a number of people occupying contiguous space – may be an accident of time and situation, in which case it is better described as a collection. The main difference is that a group has been formed or adapted for a purpose because, in the baldest possible terms, number is essential for the performance of the task.

A second obvious factor is economic – the advantage of scale. If a number of people require the same service, in many cases it is an economic use of scarce, probably specialist resources, to offer the service to them as some form of group. Herein lies the basis of the associative form of group discussed earlier as group-as-context. It is equally applicable to information-giving groups, some learning groups and others where many can be put in contact with a scarce necessary resource at the same time.

In a way the number aspect recurs in another very commonly accepted group use, that of support. Confirmation of beliefs and ideas, of actions and behaviour, a sense of belonging and of being accepted by others is, in a very basic way, a question of number. But like the essential definition of a group it also contains some aspect of commonality and of purpose. Fundamentally such support harks back once more to the basic fear of recognition of isolation, but, more than this, support, again in its number aspect, provides power. That unity gives strength has been a precept for as long as man has existed.

Then in our search we are faced with the concepts of pooling and sharing. These are perhaps best expressed in the economic thesis of division of labour. Human beings have long exploited their differences, of strength, intelligence, skill, aptitude and knowledge, so that in combination they have been able to achieve what was impossible to the individual. The catalogue of tasks which can be better performed by groups than by individuals has long been a matter of heated discussion in some areas, but it would seem that the closer the task comes to being creative, in its truest sense, the less effectively it can be performed by a group. Creativity is indeed a highly individual activity but executive processes which arise from the creative act in order to give it existence are well within the competence of group operation.

Another aspect of this pooling of difference is that it tends to be overlooked in favour of similarity, but both are important aspects of a group and they are jointly covered in the idea of comparison. One of the main problems of human existence is that of making sufficient sense of it to adopt a functionally effective modus operandi. So, though no absolute proof exists that our procedures are based on 'real' facts or understanding, we adopt those procedures which appear to work and they become an essential and integrated programme until such time as circumstances show them to be inadequate – by which time the programming tends to be so ingrained that to bring it into conscious thought and restructure it or develop new procedures becomes extremely difficult, if not actually impossible.

Comparison of our behaviour, ideas and so on with those of others offers both the comfort of finding similarity and the spur to possible change, together with the suggestion of the direction and intensity that this might take. There is of course a prerequisite for the process of comparison to be able to yield such beneficial results and that is that the individual must have some respect for those with whom he compares himself. Strangely this respect does not necessarily have to be accompanied by affection, but it does need to be based on accepting behaviour as a form of standard. Thus similarity offers comfort, confirmation and a reduction of isolation, while difference offers the opportunity of growth and increased choice.

From what has been said so far it must be clear that underlying all aspects of group benefit is the factor of number, the simple inalienable fact that increasing the number of people involved in a situation must increase at least the possibility, and often indeed the fact, of support. It likewise increases the economic use of scarce resources and the uses of difference and comparison. Strictly speaking this is a simplification. It is not the use of these factors which increases with number but their potential availability. What is required for their use is, first, a recognition that they exist, second, a willingness to use them for specific ends and, third, the designing of an effective method of use. In essence these three factors constitute the basis of any definition of groupwork. Resource theory therefore starts from the social nature of human existence. By implication groups are the essential nurturing system of human beings and the whole maturation and socialising process takes place within such systems, however small or large.

The only admissible categorisation of groups at this basic level is one that distinguishes between 'naturally' occurring groups and 'artificial' groups which, by definition, are those which have a large element of conscious and deliberate design about them, though they are dependent upon the same programming as that inculcated by a natural group. The main reason for accepting this dichotomy of groups is the fact that it exists as a perception, and a very profoundly and strongly held one, in the minds of most people. It is possible to redefine the dichotomy as an aspect of choice by indicating that natural groups, or groups accepted as natural, occur with little in the way of choice while artificial groups are created by an act of choice.

Thus it is better to accept an existing distinction between natural and artificial groups while recognising that this does not prevent any existing natural group being adapted to groupwork use and thus introducing an element of so-called artificiality. Indeed this process can clearly be seen to operate in the work of family therapists. It is also possible to see this process in groups which have been accepted as being largely natural, by which is meant created for what are universally regarded as natural purposes, as with work groups, friendship groups and so on. Therefore, as our main concern is with groupwork as a practical activity, the dichotomy is better expressed as that between created groups and adapted groups. The whole question of leadership has bedevilled groupwork from its earliest days. In essence the problem resides in another dichotomy, in this case one of philosophy. On one side of the argument stand those who believe that human beings can be directed into making change and development, that choices can be made for them, exemplars offered, information given and above all power and influence exerted with lasting effect. On the other side stand those who admit that some change may be brought about in this fashion but that it tends to be either transient or dependent upon continuous nurture or pressure; this group maintains that change, growth and development can only become a permanent fact if the change has been willingly wrought by the individual. This side of the argument states quite categorically that all that others can do for an individual is to lead him to a recognition of a need, to offer guidance on what might be done, and how, then to stay to support the individual as they actually set about instigating the required change.

The problem for groupworkers is that both points of view are valid. Thus resource theory offers what might appear to be a compromise for the practising groupworker but which is actually a pragmatic acceptance of what exists, the definition of associative patterns. These are forms of combination which embody not just the polar ends of the philosophical divide discussed above but also other matters: first, in any one group a pure form of either associative pattern may exist all the time; second, at given times during the existence of a group one pattern may be more appropriate than another and thus a pattern of the pragmatic use of both forms can exist; third, it is possible to see that one associative form may be the basis for the early stages of a group which is then progressively developed into the second associative form as the appropriate ability emerges in the group. The names given to these associative patterns, group-as-context and group-as-instrument, are clumsy, but in essence they serve to express the fundamental point. At its most basic the 'group-as-context' label delineates the idea that the group is the setting or milieu for the application and use of a scarce specialist resource, while the 'group-as-instrument' phrase denotes a system in which the unit of operation is not a specific leader, but the group itself.

A combination of the systems is quite clearly much more readily adaptable to real circumstances for the majority of groups, in that few groups need or can sustain a pure form. One other factor has to be mentioned here and that is outcome. Once more a dichotomy is found, this time between those who believe that all group outcomes result in the growth, development and change of the individual to a greater or lesser extent and those who regard the outcome as essentially the binding of the individual into membership of a unit. It is axiomatic that the second is more frequently found in the group-as-instrument situation, but the former is usually found in either state or even in a mixed associative form.

Having defined the forms of groups and leadership in these broad terms it remains to adduce precisely what they are designed to foster or achieve. As we have seen, the most basic advantage that groups offer is the fact of number, from which can be derived the potential advantage of the economic use of scarce resources, support and the uses of difference and of similarity. As all these potential factors constitute possible advantage they can equally be described as assets or resources. In order for these assets or resources to be used they have first to be brought into a situation where they can be recognised, made accessible and ultimately used. As the assets or resources are not only those possessed by individuals but also those which only emerge under conditions of cooperative combination, the absolutely basic reason for the creation or adaptation of groups is unequivocally established.

But, as has been noted earlier, that basic condition is of itself not necessarily or even likely to be effective without additional conditions being created. So we come to the ways in which these secondary but very important conditions can be brought into existence. By far the simplest method of approaching this problem is to ascertain what, in individual group circumstances, are those factors or conditions which prevent the free emergence of resources for group and individual use. It must be abundantly clear that in any associative group form composed of different individuals there will be obstacles to resource discovery and use. If this were not so, then each individual could have had available the resources needed or at least could have had some knowledge of what was required. It must be remembered that resource deficit is not the only stumbling block to appropriate performance; there is also the factor of ignorance of the existence of assets and also of the appropriate use of timing, frequency, locus of application, intensity or kind.

Resource theory thus offers some consideration of what obstacles are most commonly found to the location and use of resources in groups, because the removal, diminution or bypassing of these obstacles is the essential requirement for the freeing of resources for use. The recognition of obstacles is the basis of groupwork techniques. Once this fact is accepted, the groupwork process becomes one of logic. It also becomes one in which the skills of observation and of acquisition of the right kind of knowledge about resources and probable obstacles are of equal importance.

The process of groupwork then becomes one of matching. Given that it is possible to ascertain that one or more basic attributes of a group are regarded as essential to bring about change, development or growth to known individuals, the associative form of the required group should emerge, with the leadership form and techniques being based almost entirely upon dealing with the obstacles, which are at that stage perceived to exist, to the access to and use of appropriate resources.

At this stage it is appropriate to reconsider the second thesis of this book, which is that of influence. Because the essential skills of the groupworker are those which relate to recognising need, convening groups, removing, diminishing and bypassing obstacles to resource use and to terminating or transferring a group so that newly acquired growth, change or development is annealed and not dissipated, the aspect of insidious influence is a factor of great importance. It must be clear that, if a groupworker thinks in terms of moral imperatives, such a worker will seek directly or indirectly to bring about their implementation. The whole basis of the resource theory of groupwork most clearly lies in the generation of the recognition of much larger areas of potential choice than would otherwise exist. This does not exclude the prospect of direction, but it does require that such direction should be explicit, acknowledged and open. Choice does not actually exist when what is on offer is not understood.

Ultimately the groupworker's skill lies in his knowledge of the creation and adaptation of groups and in the application of the methods by which people can be held in groups and of the ways by which obstacles to the application of resources to beneficial ends may be removed or diminished. The final skill resides in knowing how to seal in the knowledge, growth and/or change which resource use has achieved, so that it becomes an integrated part of the individual and, in some cases, of the total group.

What, then, is different? Essentially the difference is in the provision of a universal focus for groupwork activity. For example, all the concepts which are normally offered as the aims of specific forms of groupwork, treatment, learning, empowerment, support, individual growth, change and so on, are usually backed by some borrowing from other disciplines like psychology, sociology, religion or politics about the ways in which these aims should be achieved. What is different is the recognition that all these sources of information, ideologies or beliefs about the way in which the stated aims may be achieved are subsumed under the ubiquitous requirement to locate, release and use resources. What is different is that, if this fundamental concept of resource use is applied, the coercive factor of all approaches becomes diminished as it becomes subservient to the appropriate resource use. It is no longer important for the analytical psychological groupworker that individuation is achieved through the group recognising the myths and the effects of the unconscious. It is only important that the individual group member be freed to use those resources of the group which are appropriate to his individual need; whether those resources are labelled 'collective unconscious' or not is almost irrelevant and at best any relevance of the label will reside in the individual's acceptance of it as an appropriate description of what is occurring.

There is much here that bears a striking resemblance to the need to offer a language to people to enable them to explain to themselves in a satisfactory way what is happening, so that understanding may be enhanced. As long as the trap is avoided of appearing to describe someting as if it actually had an independent existence in the form described, such descriptions can be truly seen as part of the struggle to generate practical resources, whether of an informational, feeling, behavioural or material kind.

Having stated as lucidly as possible the concepts of resource theory, we think it appropriate now to offer in total the propositions which have appeared at the end of the previous chapters including proposition 6, which refers to groupwork in general as a brief shorthand summary of this chapter. After this it is necessary to show, as far as is possible, what effect the acceptance of resource theory might have on the design and process of groups now in common use, and finally to consider the possible modifications resource theory might entail in the training and education of groupworkers.

Summary of propositions

1. Man is a social animal.
1a. Because groups have been and are instrumental in creating and in maintaining the individual in all aspects of his life, it is logical that created or adapted groups should be used as the means to support, reshape, educate or change the life style of individuals in a conscious and planned way to beneficial ends.
2. There are two definable forms of groupwork groups: 'created' and 'adapted'.
2a. A group is *created* for groupwork purposes by the coming together of a number of individuals for a shorter or longer period of time, this coming and being together constituting a fundamental and necessary condition for the achievement of their goals and one which occurs under the aegis of a groupwork convenor or convenors.
2b. A group is *adapted* to groupwork purposes when an already existing group, created, formed or arising for purposes other than those of groupwork, is entered by a groupworker or groupworkers with the intent of working with the members of that group to achieve specific groupwork ends.
3. Consciously created or adapted groups may take either of two polar forms defined by the nature of the associative patterns involved: instrumental or contextual.
3a. The *instrumental* associative form of a group occurs when the principal requirement of the group is to have access to and use of the collective resources possessed by and available to its members, known as the 'assembly effect' (Collins and Guetzkow, 1964, p. 58).

3b. The *contextual* associative form of a group occurs when the principal requirement of the group is for its members as individuals to gain access to and to use a scarce individual resource.

3c. The polar positions of instrumental and contextual associative patterns may lie on a continuum of such patterns.

3d. A group during its existence may exhibit different associative patterns at different times.

3e. Both instrumental and contextual associative group forms may be either created or adapted.

4. The factor of value in human groups lies in the individual and collective resources possessed by and available to the gestalt of group members and leader.

4a. The principal generative factor of that value is the creation of 'difference in similarity' or 'complementarity'.

4b. This principle is most active in the instrumental associative group form.

4c. Another generative factor of that value is the creation of the perception of resources of special quality.

4d. This factor is most evident in the contextual associative group form.

4e. Both generative factors can occur in both group forms.

4f. The resources of individual human beings comprise the totality of their experiences, knowledge, skills, understanding, abilities, insights, imagination and feelings.

4g. Human resources may be actual, that is known and available, or potential (forgotten or not previously exercised) but probably susceptible to being developed.

5. The basis of all groupwork is to create or adapt human groups in either contextual or instrumental form or in some combination of both to generate actual and/or potential resource systems to meet the actual and/or assessed needs of group members and to remove, diminish, change or circumnavigate obstacles to the discovery, recognition, accessibility and use of those resources.

6. Groupwork is fundamentally a conscious, complex human relational process designed to match resources to needs, based upon (a) the assessment of need, (b) creating or adapting a group-unit system, (c) holding that system in existence, (d) locating actual and/or potential resources, (e) removing,

diminishing, changing or circumnavigating obstacles to the availability and use of those resources, (f) creating, sustaining and developing patterns of resource use, (g) reviewing and monitoring that use, (h) assessing the outcomes, (i) adapting to perceived group change, and (j) terminating or transforming the group.

8

Group Design I

> At best control is but one component in any program for personal improvement or social reform. . . . Changing behavior is pointless in the absence of any coherent plan for how it should be changed. (Miller, 1969)

The idea that social groupwork groups should be designed or at least have a design is somewhat alien to the profession. It also seems somewhat at odds with the process of discovering and utilising resources. That this is not so we hope to make clear as we look at the more commonly used types of groups.

Dewey (1938, p. 57), trying to explain the lack of planning in classroom control wrote: 'The causes for such lack are varied. The one which is peculiarly important to mention . . . is the idea that such advance planning is unnecessary and even that it is inherently hostile to the legitimate freedom of those being instructed.' Kurland (1978) in quoting this extract was of the opinion that the explanation Dewey offered for lack of planning was equally applicable to groupwork design. Groupwork literature has a plethora of approaches, models, types and so on which present a picture of confusion because there appears never to have been a central theme of any kind to which all these approaches could establish a relationship. Thus, as we have seen, the only common factor has been the insistence by most of those involved on the difference, that is the digital difference, between their particular production and those of everyone else. In essence these differences are analog differences rather than digital and every group which has ever been formed has as its basis some element of the exploitation of resources.

However groups are still classified, not by single criteria and variations or by distinct difference, but almost always by mixtures of both. This has led to unlikes being compared, to unlikes being constituted as parts of continua and to an essential lack of clarity about the whole process. In fact it is possible to classify groups in many ways – by the kind of service they offer, the setting in which they are used, the form of leadership which is used and so on. In 1961, for instance, Joyce Gale Klein introduced what she called 'a suggested typology, from which the selection may be made of group methods with clients in social agencies'. The typology was presented as follows:

1. leisure time groups;
2. group education
   – Family life education groups,
   – Orientation groups,
   – Pre-intake groups;
3. social group treatment
   – group treatment aimed at maintaining adaptive patterns,
   – group treatment aimed at a modification of adaptive patterns;
4. group psychotherapy.

This simple typology, early as it was in the literature of group-work, was founded on a more certain base than much of what followed. Indeed Klein believed 'that all groups display the same basic elements of process', and that the analog differences were dependent upon such factors as the purpose of the group, the system in which it was imbedded, the qualities of the members and the 'unique qualities' of the groupworker. Klein's typology is an almost pure set of categories of groupworker purpose; the only significant odd member of the system is leisure activities, which are different in that whatever groupworker purpose they may embody is not made explicit.

   Later writers, such as Pappell and Rothman in 1966, proposed a typology of groupwork which was based upon models, in Pappell and Rothman's case on three models:

1. the social goals model – the cultivation of social consciousness;
2. the remedial model – the treatment of individuals in the group context;
3. the reciprocal model – towards a system of mutual aid.

Lang (1972) said of this typology that the social goals and the remedial models were models based upon the nature of the group-worker aims and the reciprocal model was based upon process: 'The models are not cast in the same defining terms, not expressed in relation to a common supporting theory and not constructed on equivalent theoretical foundations.' Leaving aside the difficulty of combining into any typology of groups such factors as groupwork purpose, the needs of potential members, settings, activities, styles of leadership and so on, the concept of group design can only really present two very simple ideas.

1. There are known to be a whole variety of elements of group-work which are believed more or less accurately to relate to or to produce certain group outcomes.
2. As groupwork groups are essentially set up or adapted to deal with certain needs of their prospective members, the basic consideration of group design should be to provide that combination of the elements of groupwork known or believed to be the most effective in meeting those needs.

For the purpose of illustrating these two points and how the fundamental concept of resource discovery and exploitation facilitates group design, it is proposed to look at groups defined as the commonest and most frequently used groupwork groups. This is in no way a typology but merely a means of demonstrating utility.

Groupworkers, that is practitioners, tend to use three descriptive criteria when talking about the groups they run. These are the group's focus, the form the group takes and the setting in which it is held. The most usual descriptions of focus are those which refer to 'common problems' which can often be subdivided into problems of illness or disability or social condition, of support, information giving and learning. A brief survey of groupwork literature will reveal a plethora of papers, descriptions and presentations with titles containing the words 'Groupwork with . . .' followed by something denoting what might be called a problem category, such as abused children, single parents, AIDS victims and so on. The concept of common problem is clear – people, maybe of widely differing backgrounds, abilities and so on, who are all, at a given time, discovered to have in common a 'so-called' problem of illness, disability or social condition.

Group design which is focused on a 'common problem'

In looking at the pure form of the common problem focus as a starting-point it should be made clear what the usually accepted criteria for creating or, much more infrequently, adapting, such a group are. The first, without doubt, is concerned with removing the sense of uniqueness that each individual may possess. The discovery that others have the same or similar problem or difficulty, while possessing some probable negative aspects, also possesses the positive potential of generating not just a sense of relief that one is not peculiarly alone, but also the expectation of some understanding based upon first-hand and personal experience. Potential common problem group members have been heard to express doubts, sometimes very strongly, that a group of peers would be any good and to say that what they really required was an 'expert' who knew more about their particular problem than 'ordinary' people. There is some comfort to be derived from a realisation by an individual that even those they would normally consider to be more socially competent than themselves are equally in need of help to deal with some particular difficulties.

The second and equally important factor relates to the perception that, because the individuals with the same problem *are* individual and thus in many ways uniquely different, for example in the way they regard the common problem and in the methods by which they have attempted to deal with it, their successes and failures are also different. Indeed that difference, in that it begins to demonstrate alternatives hitherto not even contemplated, becomes, or can become, one of the most important resources available to the group.

It now becomes clear that, if these resources are to be exploited for the mutual benefit of the group members, the way that the group is 'designed', its modus operandi, must be of paramount concern. For example, if all the potential members of a group have a marked similarity in a great part of their biographical backgrounds and in their abilities, there is no doubt that the reduction of isolation uniqueness will occur, but this may well be fundamentally negative in effect and depressing rather than positive and relieving. In order to exploit resources it is seldom adequate just to assemble a group of individuals purely on the basis of a common problem focus. Exploitable difference which can give rise to an increase in available alternative strategies of coping is a much more valuable concept. But within the common problem focus other factors occur, each of which can be regarded as the basis of a unique focus. Thus support, information giving and learning may be included. For instance, a common problem focus group which has exploitable differences in its members already possesses the possibility of benefiting from information exchange. The mere presentation by individuals of their experience can constitute a form of information giving for other members. Such information often has those most positive attributes of being readily assimilable, relevant, believable and based on credible experience.

Specialist information may also be available to such a group through the medium of the groupworker or through imported individual inputs. These, unless very carefully aimed, may well have fewer positive attributes, because material is often derivative, cumulative and theoretically oriented. As has already been suggested, the expertise of the groupworker in this matter of design must be based very firmly on a knowledge of, and skill, in the creation and adaptation of groups in ways which are most conducive to eliciting and using those resources, mainly within the group itself, but also probably in some measure external to it, which will produce the most enhancing benefit for the group members. The power, the benefit, the skill of the groupworker resides in his ability and knowledge in creating and holding appropriate group structures.

A group with a common problem focus may well have the group-as-context form, in which case the group leader will have had an expectation that the major need of the group members is to be offered a form of expert knowledge and understanding as the most important resource. As we have seen, this is not entirely the one-way resource use it appears to be. Even the most sophisticated and apparently appropriate expert resource is of minimal value if the recipients do not possess the resource ability to learn and benefit from it. Many an information giver has learnt to his chagrin that material most obviously necessary to a group of recipients has proven to be absolutely useless because the resource base to which it was presented was not adequate to the task of assimilating it. This is most commonly stated as the fact that, for new information to be taken up and used, it must possess two factors, relevance, as perceived by the recipients, and clear and demonstrable links to what they already know.

In the group-as-context form a common problem focus group has a design which contains some development of appropriate belief in the major group resource, that is in the group leader. In this respect all such groups need an element of the group-as-instrument associative pattern in order that credibility and need may be established. Significantly the more essential the information and understanding required from the major resource, the greater the threat involved, the more the associative pattern needs to be that of closeness and support.

All common problem focus groups are concerned with learning. As we have seen, the coping strategies which people have developed for themselves are limited by many factors which are often but little understood. Tramlining, which appears to describe the way in which individuals are held to what might be defined as a predestined selection of behaviour patterns, makes the perception of alternatives almost impossible. But learning takes time. There has to be first of all the presentation of material, of ideas, of information. This has to be followed by the assimilation of the information and the perception of its relevance and utility. This in turn must be followed by the attempt to practise what has been gained to ensure that the new ideas and so on can form the basis of new and relevant behaviour.

In all this the groupworker will have needed to design a group, in terms of the selection of members, the frequency of sessions and the total life of the group, which will allow for the discovery and presentation of resources, their use and practice, given the needs and abilities of the group members. A very relevant example of this process is to be found in the kind of groupwork workshop described below. This followed the usual pattern of group-as-context developing into group-as-instrument.

Example

One of the bonuses of groupwork workshops has always been the exchange of information which takes place. A collection of people usually already involved in working with groups come together with an experienced groupworker to explore the problems they are experiencing and to seek for and discuss ways of coping.

For instance, a group of residential workers started their three-day session immediately after introductions with brief descriptions of the kind of work they were doing. More especially they concentrated on the groups they worked with and their successes and their problems. Because every member in the group workshop was in a roughly similar situation – indeed they were all employed by the same authority – each statement had particular relevance.

It did not take much in the way of encouragement for the group members to realise that here for the taking were new ideas, different techniques, assets and resources, not the ephemera of words, but credible people. They might have unresolved problems in their own world of work but the striking fact was that each group member tended to have attempted to cope with problems with which others were still struggling. Of course there were differences of emphasis, personality and support; nevertheless the information take-up was high. What is more, the initial contact having been made during the workshop, the different individual resources of information remained available by telephone and visit to monitor, assist and comment long after the workshop had closed.

In this instance, once brought together under the aegis of a credible leader and held by being given a structure and procedure which made much of their expertise and experience, firstly as complementary to that of the leader but ultimately as of prime importance, the group were freed to express their ideas and experiences. The realisation that others were not only interested but needed their help created resource use which continued long after the workshop had run its course. If we examine this closely the elements of design are clearly apparent.

Firstly the groupwork leader had three essential credits, experience, knowledge and, most fundamentally, an understanding of group behaviour. Secondly the group were selected not so much on the basis that they were all in the same line of work but that they had all reached a point in that work where they knew that there were things that they needed to know. They were also selected on the basis of the fact that the group leader was aware that they had demonstrated different ways of coping with some of the problems they faced. Thus the resource pool was not only larger but also diverse. The method of gaining access was simple:

(1) to demonstrate and confirm the wide knowledge and experience of the group leader and thus enhance or generate credibility; (2) as trust and security developed, to encourage the development of the credibility of group members for each other by generating the opportunity to make visible the resources they possessed; and (3) for the leader to become one of the contributing members of the groupwork workshop offering a wider perspective than most and to encourage the development of a continuing support system amongst the group members during the period of their attempts to establish the new learning as action.

The common problem in this group may not have been as obvious as some but it was a common 'need to know'. The point that each member had reached was essentially a sticking-point, beyond which they could not go without help. Essentially they sought that help through the medium of contact with a specialist resource and the group-as-context form arose. Eventually they developed the group-as-a-whole as a resource and the group-as-instrument was born.

It must be obvious, as has been stressed throughout, that the pure form of associative patterns and of group focus is nearly always diluted by other patterns and forms, sometimes sequentially, as in the illustration just given, sometimes intermittently. Nevertheless group design should always be based quite clearly on the nature and accessibility of the resources which are to be used to meet and execute the needs of the group and its members.

Finally it is necessary to consider what were the major obstacles to resource access and use in this particular group. In the first instance there was the basic idea that the learning that was needed in order to be able to cope with particular difficulties that each group member was experiencing could only come from some credible expert. This was reinforced by the relatively low value that all the workers placed upon their own knowledge and skill. After all, what was most obvious to them all was that although they had achieved certain goals other aspects of their groups were stagnant, if not deteriorating, and they did not know how such problems could be dealt with.

Thus the first and most important obstacle was to clarify the role of the specialist and the value of the group members' own experience and knowledge. The technique used was relatively simple but was exclusively based on a straightforward process of obstacle removal. In the process of introduction each member was invited to talk briefly about their work and in particular the kind of problems they were dealing with. This information was supplied in reference to the leader's statement that the material the group could best work with would be that which arose from their own practice and whatever progress they could make would automatically be available for practical application in the areas from which the original material came.

The second technique which was applied as material became available was concerned with the logical processes of problem solving; in other words a demonstrable process of structuring thoughts, impressions and information was offered and the members were encouraged to apply this to the material that was emerging and then adapt it to their own needs.

Ultimately the group leader became the resource to which members would turn when they were not quite sure what method or sequence of techniques was appropriate to order the material they were getting. The other major resources were, of course, being provided by the members themselves and it never ceases to amaze me that people working within a few miles of one another and for the same organisation and in similar capacities actually have so little contact with each other. Members were constantly realising that, having been brought into face-to-face contact, knowledge and experience were available in abundance merely for the asking. Once members had seen demonstrated the value of their own material the exchange of problems, solutions, ideas and so on was self-energising.

The final obstacle was that, without support, much of the acquired knowledge and skill would atrophy or be overwhelmed by the pressure of ordinary, everyday events. This was dealt with in two ways, by converting the group into a support system with a forward programme of contact and visits and by providing an information and advice system to which all had access more or less at will.

Not all common problem groups have the advantage enjoyed by this one, which was that all the members had a realisation that they were stuck and most were remarkably clear that they needed help to proceed. The willingness to suffer what they could well have envisaged as an embarrassing exposure of their groupwork deficiencies was a very powerful motivation which was the prime instrument used by the group leader to overcome the remaining obstacles.

One final point must be that many people are not averse to sharing their knowledge and skills with others. The important obstacle is not secrecy; it is the simple fact that people just do not think of the possibility of such an exchange of material. The very act of communication with others, other than with immediate friends, seems to be the last ploy that comes to mind. Much can be made of the intense dislike, amounting to fear, that many have of appearing to be ignorant or not wholly self-sufficient. This may be an even more potent factor amongst those professionals who cherish a faultless image in the mistaken belief that others expect them to be professionally omnicompetent and omniscient.

Group design which has the focus of treatment

The traditional groupwork method envisions therapists as highly directive, especially during the early phases of treatment. The therapist engages in diagnosis, at both the individual and group levels, continuously throughout the course of treatment. He also formulates both short-term and long-term objectives for individual members and for the group as a whole, and he engages in a series of systematic, direct interventions to attain those objectives. (Feldman and Wodarski, 1975, p. 10)

Feldman and Wodarski postulate a high degree of direction by the therapist/groupworker in the formation of a treatment group, thus putting this form of group firmly into the group-as-context associative pattern, with the major resource being the group leader.

The basic assumptions behind the design of such a group are quite simply that some specific deficiency of or on the part of the group members can be wholly or partially remedied by their being exposed to a worker with the knowledge and technical expertise in the ways of encouraging take-up and use of that knowledge. The resources which the members bring to the group are thus often assumed to be those associated with normal patterns of learning and their attendant individual motivation and intent. Philosophically the basic idea is the simple one that it is possible for individuals to learn new patterns of behaviour, to acquire new skills and to achieve new forms of understanding. This, of course, has to be based upon the assumption that it is possible for a groupworker or teacher to acquire a reasonable understanding of individual deficiencies and needs and to plan and execute a programme to meet them.

Fundamental to all treatment programmes, though often well obscured by the perceptions of the power and skill which group members hold of group leaders, is the absolute necessity for what is offered to be able to be taken up, adapted to idiosyncratic individual ability and ultimately used. It is a commonplace of teaching that, before new and different knowledge can become a usable addition to what an individual already possesses, it is necessary to establish acceptable links between new and old and if possible to demonstrate the utility or superiority of the new. In this way the cost/reward ratio may well be tipped in favour of the amount of effort required to put take-up and absorption, transformation and use into effect.

There is also the factor that sometimes the unlearning of the old knowledge is a prerequisite to acquiring the new, though many have pointed out that individuals are very capable of holding contradictory and mutually exclusive viewpoints, ideas and opinions and behaviour patterns simultaneously without concern until a situation occurs which brings previously ignored conflict into high relief.

In the case of the treatment group the design has to take cognisance of two major areas of resource availablity: first, the resources which the therapist/groupworker can be expected to possess and, second, the specific member resources, which may be roughly categorised as the ability to utilise external resources – that is, an initial ability to absorb what is being offered at some level.

In a paper on the group treatment of chronic sorrow, Engebrigsten and Heap (1988) indicated that the major themes of their work were in the areas of group process and group content. These major themes can be listed as follows:

Group process themes
- support through mutual identification,
- group identity and cohesion,
- ventilation and self-confrontation,
- reality maintenance.

Group content themes
- impact on family culture and organisation,
- ways of coping,
- the loneliness of caring,
- uncertainty,
- the treatment experience,
- ambivalence towards the sick child.

The resources which the groupworker brings to this kind of situation may be very simply stated as his own knowledge of the problem area and his knowledge and skill in generating and maintaining a group system in which the resources of the group members are located and used, including their ability to use those of the groupworker and of other external sources. In order to examine those resources it must be stated clearly at the outset that the concept of treatment is concerned with the application of some action to one person by another. In other words it is a positive action directed toward another person. Thus the emphasis on the role of the groupworker is natural.

If we look at the themes in the content section above, largely because in terms of order they are more likely to appear earlier in the group than the process themes, it can be seen that at the surface level what the groupworker is aiming to do is to offer information. At a deeper level he is also establishing credibility, a process which we know depends almost exclusively upon perception over time by group members.

Credibility in this case depends upon the worker's ability to demonstrate understanding of group members' problems and difficulties at the level at which they appear to exist for those members and also to place them within the wider understanding of such problems, which is both cumulative and structured experience and also theoretical. One of the major factors of this situation tends to lie in the perception by the members that the groupworker is a person who not only has seen the beginning of their problems but has also seen the ending. Though at one remove from the actual experience, he has available a perspective of time and probability of occurrence which most likely is not a significant part of the wisdom of the group members. In this context the timescales are a prime example of the specialised knowledge that a groupworker may use. It is common knowledge that even trivial problems are a great deal more devastating in their effects if the duration of their existence is not known or, even worse, if the outcome is the subject of highly inaccurate 'traditional' knowledge. For instance, in the example given by Engebrigsten and Heap, the impact of the recognition of a probable terminal illness, or even of continued deterioration on family culture and organisation, is a matter of horizon-filling consequence to the individuals who comprise a family and is also very largely idiosyncratic. What the groupworker has to offer as a resource is an understanding of this problem which is general and not idiosyncratic and which is related to a knowledge of a multiplicity of ways of coping – all this related to a timescale which, however roughly delineated, has the effect of charting a series of steps into what may well have been an essentially unmapped and desperately frightening future.

Uncertainty may well remain, but there are some markers along the path, and the knowledge that others have been there before has connotations which can take some of the edge off uncertainty. It is equally important that the groupworkers can be understood to have seen others take this journey. The application of treatment is based upon the possession of this kind of knowledge, knowledge in the sense of knowing some relatively concrete facts. When treatment programmes are explained at the beginning of group formation, such knowledge should be displayed, albeit often in a very basic way. It has frequently been my experience that groupworkers have set up 'treatment' groups with no very clear idea of the resources they might need to possess and use for it to become a viable situation. The result is often that the information which is an essential in the establishment of credibility is missing or at best obscure. It is possible to help without this basic informational resource, but the help then becomes what we will consider in relation to the process themes, that is the development of a system which allows and promotes recognition of, and access to, member resources. But this is not then a treatment group, in that the most essential component of a treatment group is the resource, residing in the groupworker, of special knowledge.

Of course, in the interests of clarity, process and content themes have been separated. In reality this is not a matter of sequence but of dominance. The primary resource of the groupworker's special knowledge and of the ability to give relevant information is only theoretically separable from the process of beginning to create a group system. Having shown that, although the family situation is idiosyncratic and individual, it is also in another sense not unique. Also where there are similarities to the experience of others and to the structured knowledge of the problem, a situation can be created in which the sharing and mutual support of group members becomes not only possible but highly probable.

In the example under discussion here, Engebrigsten and Heap refer to the 'rich supportive resource' which they believe resides in the common experience of the families they are working with. This is an extension of a common human experience, that of seeking for things in common with those with whom we are thrown into contact, especially if the circumstances and the people are both unfamiliar. But this is a safety-seeking ploy and what a treatment group needs is not just safety but difference, which can be translated into credible extensions of understanding and behaviour, into modifications of attitude, changes of opinion and into the development of new understanding. As the group begins to discover the safety levels which exist, it becomes possible for the expression of emotion to take place because it has become apparent that such an activity is acceptable and probably even expected: 'One perceives an item of information, one understands it and assimilates it; and this results in change and generalisation. This self-analysis brings with it an implicit change of attitude' (Torras, 1989/90, p. 257).

Torras also separates content and process by referring to two different levels of group. In level one the worker gives information and guidance. The groups in this case are those formed by the parents of drug-taking children, so the information concerns the effects of drugs, the nature of drug-taking habits, basic concepts of drug taking and instruction about the known effective ways of talking to addicted children about drugs. Torras maintains that this information produces individuals who are more knowledgeable and probably more realistic. They are then ready to move into a level two group which is based on the gains of level one and helps the family to bring about structural changes in the supportive atmosphere of the group. There is some considerable element of self-help in this stage of the group treatment.

If the resources of the groupworker are the dominant factor in groups specifically oriented towards treatment it cannot be forgotten that they are by no means the only resources which are required. It must be obvious that in our consideration of worker resources it has not been possible to avoid the necessity of commenting on the essential requirement of member resources. Indeed Torras hinted that a large element of self-help was involved in treatment groups, a fact to which we will return later.

It has been clearly stated that the process of information giving serves to set the individual group member's problems into a wider, structured context and gives hope that the way ahead has been travelled before and that there are landmarks and timescales. But to be effective in creating this structure information has to be such that it is assimilable within the context of the recipient's world, which must lead to a consideration of those design elements which, by unnecessarily emphasising the content expertise of the worker, can lead to the development of a dependent state.

It is a very fine calculation indeed to know what amount of display of expertise is required to generate safety without so diminishing other resource use – the group member's own – before dependency comes into being. The balance changes as the group-worker and the group members change. It must also be calculated differently for different potential group members, depending largely upon their need for security and upon their ability to grasp the information offered and to begin to recognise and use the resources available to them. Thus the design of treatment groups, like that of all groups, is based upon an assessment of the resources immediately available and upon the time and methods which may be necessary to gain access to other potential resources.

It is now necessary to look at two factors which have only been touched upon so far, namely the dominance of information giving or group building and the element of self-help which may exist in even the most leader-dominanted groups. The domination of information giving in the early stages of some treatment groups is directly related to the clarity with which the problem or focus of treatment is understood. In a sense this means both placing the individual experience into the wider context of the general and meeting deficiencies in knowledge and understanding.

There is a need to understand that the self-help factor referred to earlier takes place only in treatment groups in which the powerful contextual formation is relaxed for group members to interact with one another beyond the simple effect of contagion; that is, of being witness to something which has a direct and immediate connection with and value to one's own state. This relaxation is consonant with some deviation from the absolute contextual design which implies that the focus of treatment is the individual. What spin-off occurs in such a group is an important factor in creating the group in the first instance, but it remains dramatically less than the direct benefit of expertise to the individual member. However this basic disregard of the resources of members which is built into the design of contextual groups has yielded quite considerably owing to the increase in understanding of the concepts of peer credibility and similarity of experience and also of the value of peer support systems.

Thus a prime design consideration must rest upon the assessment of the original ability of potential group members, firstly for security, in the sense of being able to trust a credible leader, secondly as regards their need for and ability to accept and use information and knowledge, and thirdly as to their competence in sharing, which is necessary in order to broaden the basis of understanding and of action possibilities.

That these assessments are very difficult to make with any considerable degree of accuracy is one very valid reason for contractual obligations to contain an unequivocal assertion of the necessity of renegotiation as and when additional information emerges which alters the original assessment. Also, as the safety element may be of paramount importance and because most groups have a much stronger element of directive leadership in their formative stages, treatment groupworkers have a need to take these factors into consideration when making their original design. Ultimately the treatment group design must show a balance between the resource factors involved, namely between the problem-oriented expertise of the leader, his expertise in group formation, holding and development, and the individual and collective resource systems of the group members which have a focus on individual and/or group benefit.

9

Group Design II

Self-help groups, then, are much more than meetings of fellow sufferers. They provide a focus for people with similar problems to meet and share their experience and problems, and their ways of coping. They can be centres of social regeneration where individuals who feel isolated and stigmatised can gain strength together to deconstruct their shared problems and reconstruct their lives. (Robinson, 1980)

Robinson earlier (1977) listed the main characteristics of self-help groups, as follows:

1. the common experience of members,
2. the development of mutual help and support,
3. the development of the helper principle,
4. the exercise of mutual reinforcement of position,
5. the exercise of collective will power and belief,
6. the sharing of information,
7. the exercise of constructive action towards shared goals.

It must be clear from this list that self-help groups possess at least one characteristic in common with common problem groups, and indeed the self-help process is in essence the extreme example of the group-as-instrument associative pattern, in the same way that the treatment group is the extreme example of the group-as-context associative pattern.

Group design which takes the form of the self-help group

The title of 'self-help group' tends to sit badly with the idea of

126

design with its implications of planning and rightness of fit, but although such groups represent the absolute extreme point of resource use it is still essential to recognise that resources are not immediately available just because they are needed. The whole thesis of this book is founded upon the idea that resources need a system in which they can manifest themselves, not least because the resources come from multiple individual sources, but also because the recognition of resource presence, potential and value is frequently absent. So when self-help groups are somewhat glibly referred to as free from professional expertise, there is as little reason for this to be a true statement of fact as the comment that human intervention can be wholly objective.

What is important is that the creation of a self-help group has to be brought about in such a way that the dependence of the group members on the creator is minimal and is thereafter reduced even further. Thus, as Levy (1976, p. 321) remarks in his definition of the self-help group, 'its origins and sanctions for existence rest with the members of the group themselves rather than with some external agency or authority'.

A groupworker responsible for creating a self-help group must still be concerned with the first two essential aspects of group formation: that a visible need exists and that a group composed in a particular way can provide some of the resources necessary to meet that need. But even more important than usual in this process is the need for the groupworker to be acutely aware that his skill lies very much in the acts of group creation and guidance and much less in intervention or in specialist problem knowledge. Indeed it may be helpful to draw an analogy of the potential group members with employers who are asking a professional to design some construction for them, advise them as to what form it should best take and how it might well operate; but it will ultimately be entirely controlled by those who employed the designer in the first instance. The analogy may be taken even further in that the designer may well accept the role of maintenance engineer, to be available as and when requested.

To quote Levy again, a self-help group 'relies upon its own members' efforts, skill and knowledge and concern as its primary source of help, with the structure of the relationships between members being one of peers so far as help-giving and support are concerned'. Levy also comments on the fact that members of such a group,' may in turn draw upon professional guidance'. Matzat (1989/90) wrote: 'The positive effects are made possible by the exchange of very personal experiences, the possibility of empathy, solidarity and social support. People help one another in turn, and serve each other as models of effective ways of coping with common problems.' And again, 'The participants in self-help groups are both producers and consumers of psycho-social services.'

Priestley *et al.* (1978), writing about discussion groups, indicated that the major advantages of such groups were very similar to those of self-help groups:

1. motivation – 'the presence of other people with similar problems which they wish to tackle is a powerful motivating factor';
2. shared experience – the most common way that people acquire their information, values and attitudes in ordinary life situations;
3. insight – this is generated by the exposure of individual experience to the scrutiny of others in a way which is not common experience;
4. mutual support – group membership tends to promote a willingness to work with and to help others.

Garvin (1981) reminds us that a self-help group 'challenges professional self-importance', so it is appropriate to look more closely at exactly what the principles which underlie self-help groups may be and why they appear to some professionals to be in conflict with their professional ideals. It can be established that self-help groups appear to operate in two large spheres of activity; that is to say there are two major design forms. The first focuses upon member change within the group system and the second focuses upon creating change outside the group system.

Focus A: internal change
Sharing by giving support and information and generating conditions for change

A1. Member change by modifying or controlling behaviours and attitudes	A2. Member change by adapting to or coping with a condition or catastrophic event

Focus B: external change
By creating a change in circumstances outside the group

Most members of Focus A self-support groups have problems which often attract hostility and lack of understanding from the general public, together with a very powerful feeling that no one actually understands what having or being such a problem is like until they have personal experience of it. This is probably the basis for the rejection, so often expressed, of the 'expert'. Nevertheless there is a role for the expert whose expertise lies in an ability to help create self-help groups and which is founded on a clear knowledge of what is required and, more importantly, what is not required.

Any analysis of the design elements of self-help groups must start, as always, with aims and obstacles – more particularly the latter. A prominent obstacle of many self-help groups seems to be the reluctance of potential members to accept that they have a problem or that they are a problem. Indeed many self-help groups start with some form of confrontation with new members which is specifically designed to dispose of the common perception members have of being a victim and of believing that the responsibility for their current state can be laid anywhere except at their own door.

Once ownership of the problem or state has been accepted, the next stage must be clarification. This is a major step in the dismantling of the personal myth which each member has constructed as a protective device in order to put some kind of individually acceptable explanation upon what they know is happening or has happened to them. Because this explanation tends to be a myth, and thus inaccurate, it has to be got rid of before a better and more rational and accurate explanation can be established. This second large obstacle is met from the combined resources of the group. Because a member has passed through the rite of induction by airing his problem, his personal story can be shown to be directly related in many areas of similarity to the stories of other group members. Both new member and group can then come to possess credibility for each other. It is at this point that the professional working with the group tends to have least credibility because of the obvious lack of practical personal experience of the focus problem of the group. Now the resources of the group, both in terms of similarity of experience and of idiosyn-cratic response, become applicable. Once again the major effect of difference of response offers the possibility of increasing the individual's repertoire of technical and practical responses, along with an enhanced understanding generated by being exposed to the emotions, thoughts and solutions of credible others.

As many of the problems which can be dealt with in self-help groups attract the opprobrium of society at large, the next obstacle concerns the realignment of self-esteem and a beginning of under-standing the knock-on effect of stigmatisation. Being accepted by others who have themselves not only survived such stigmatisation but actually restructured their lives in ways designed to negate it and also to prevent it recurring offers role models of success. The process at issue here is one of bringing about a change of percep-tion, both the individual's perception of himself and his perception of others. One of the major learning factors is the dawning realisa-tion of the way that specific behaviours and attitudes provoke responses which tend to establish a self-fulfilling prophecy and a downward spiral of self-pity.

Once the process of dismantling the mythic carapace is begun, the positive factor of building a more viable and effective person can begin. This is accomplished by the use of the resource experi-ence possessed by the group; once again difference is the crucial factor. New ways of doing things, plans for change, are available from the cumulative experience. This stage has then to develop into action which is planned and consciously undertaken in selected areas of behaviour, initially in those areas where a successful outcome has, in the opinion and experience of the group, a high rating of probable success. Rehearsal, role play, support, encouragement and a clearly defined set of goals and an equally clearly defined path to achieve them, founded upon actual collective experience, are the essentials here.

The final phase is the integration of the new behaviours and attitudes and their constant and successful use in everyday life. This process is seldom a straight line and is often marked by lapses and deviations, but behind such discontinuities lies the group, whose realistic expectations accept the probability of such occur-rences. Two factors operate here, the sense of no longer being alone and unable to cope and the feeling that the individual has obligations of honour to the group.

Of course the professional worker with knowledge of the particular problems with which the self-help group is attempting to cope, as well as precise knowledge of group creation, can provide valuable help as a resource system containing information and contacts. But as self-help groups can be the extreme example of the group-as-instrument it must be evident that the dominant and almost total resource system is that which lies in the experience and credibility of the group members. Thus it is not surprising that professionals who have been taught that their expertise is the dominant and solely reliable resource in the helping situation are often nonplussed by their rejection. But their dismay could be lessened if they were to realise that, even in the most extreme example of group-as-context and the domination by expert resource, some contribution of resources from group members is necessary if the group is not to be useless. It is the wide system of resource and the flexible response to need which constitutes effective groupwork and, whereas at one end of the spectrum it may well be true that the expert knows best, at the other the expert resource is in effect the person or persons who are the problems or who have the difficulties.

Group design, then, in this case must be almost wholly related to supplying the knowledge and skill to help create the system for the members to be able to exploit their own resources to their best advantage. The element of available specialist knowledge may be of greater value where the 'problem' is that of dramatic life change or personal catastrophe, providing better understanding and a series of markers of probable progress, together with some vital contact with other agencies.

Focus B self-help groups are usually based on the assumption that a united group of people has or can have a significantly greater influence on power structures to bring about change than isolated individuals. In essence, however small or parochial the target of such groups may be, they are pressure groups designed to give a louder, more effective voice to the needs of their members. Individuals can be ignored for many reasons, not least because the perceived consequences of ignoring them are infinitely small by comparison with the consequences which ignoring other influences may entail. But there is also the factor that many reasonable issues are ignored because they are presented in the wrong way, to the wrong people and frequently at the wrong time and place.

The power of numbers is one of the salient points about groups and in this case it is markedly important. This is so not only from the appearance of strength which number tends to create, but also from the point of view of the individual with a difficulty who can be supported and encouraged to make efforts in company which he would not or could not make alone. The sharing effect is also of paramount importance and in this context it should be noted that one of the major obstacles in such groups is produced by the effects of size and structure. Sharing becomes more difficult as group size increases. There are more ideas and experiences available, but gaining access to them becomes limited by the factors of time and opportunity. Structure is important, particularly role structure, for the collection of information and the planning of action are small-group activities, whereas the giving of information and the major effects of numbers in action are more effectively achieved in larger groups.

Specialist help may well be more useful to this kind of self-help group because some information which may be of crucial importance may not be readily available to the group. Whatever specialist help is needed there has to be a strong wish on the part of the members to effect change and the ways in which collective resources can achieve this may have to be learned. Given that such a group stays together long enough, the essential sharing process can begin to affect the feeling of benefit that members derive from the group. The thesis that those who receive should also be givers often generates in people who have seldom had cause to believe that they had anything of value to give a new sense of worth.

Group design in residential settings

Groupwork writing and thinking on both sides of the Atlantic has largely ignored group living settings. This omission is quite remarkable when one considers that the practitioner in day and residential centres almost certainly spends a much higher proportion of his or her time with groups of users than does the typical fieldworker equivalent. (Brown, 1990, pp. 269–70)

The lack of literature described by Brown stems from several known causes, one of which is that groupwork purists see the fluctuating alliances in a residential system, what Brown calls the 'mosaic' of groupings, as not conforming to their concept of a group. But this is very like believing that swans are white, therefore a black swan is not really a swan at all. The fact that there are infinitely more similarities than differences between black and white swans and between 'groups' and the 'groupings' in residential settings is ignored. As has been pointed out before, this is characteristic of the current hugely powerful trend to analyse and thus discover differences, rather than to synthesise and thus to discover underlying similarities. The essential outcome, not often foreseen, of carrying analysis in this sense too far is to make a fetish of difference in the process of creating a small field of personal influence by defining it as 'new'. In turn this diminishes the visibility of basic similarities, creates jealousy guarded boundaries and makes comparisons almost impossible. These differences are enshrined in a vocabulary and a belief system which make even more difficult any perception of the basic and common factors, thus generating practitioners whose expertise lies in one apparently distinct and separate form of practice which is not transferable to any other.

Of course, when an area of human activity is as universal as groups, a breaking down of the material about them into manageable parts for the purposes of study and understanding is essential, but in the process the fundamental similarities should never be lost sight of in the rush to create a 'new' approach by closing the boundaries around it as if it was a separate and distinct entity.

> Groups are a little like dogs. Anyone who knows nothing about dogs must surely be very puzzled by the diversity of creatures which apparently belong to the family of 'Dog'. To recognise that all these very different creatures have in fact arisen from the same basic stock is to recognise that they all have certain features in common, and the diversity arises from the fact that they have been bred for different purposes in the long association of man and dog. (Douglas, 1978, p. 20)

We are thus obliged to state that the differences between groups, groupings and all forms of human collectivity reside in the simple fact of 'breeding'. Various aspects of common group behaviour have been omitted, intensified, interpreted, prolonged, diminished and so on to fit the needs of given situations, whether these are the actual needs of that situation or the belief system of the adapter. But the most fundamental aspect of all human groupings, which may be defined as an awareness of the presence of others and the production of responses based on that awareness, exists in all of them. What follows from that is also simple: that, as the basic value of all groups is to increase the resources available for use, then even the most transient and mosaic-like of groupings must form an exploitable resource system.

If we substitute the concept of 'design' for that of 'breeding for purpose' then groups operating in a residential setting can be seen as combining the elements basic to all groups into a situation-specific pattern. It is that particular and peculiar selection and combination which constitutes the distinction of one group from another and not the elements themselves or the basic aim of resource discovery and use.

There are groups within the ambit of residential situations which have these elements combined in such a way that even the purist group theorist would accept that they were 'groups' in the terms of limited definition; that is, they are formally structured in precisely the way that groups outside the residential scene would be structured. The major defining difference would be the consequences of selecting the members of the group from a small population who are already in continuous contact with one another within defined material boundaries.

Brown (1990) offers a typology of groups and groupings in residential and day care which includes the following forms:

1. the whole community,
2. living together groups,
3. informal friendship/affinity groups,
4. groups to discuss group living issues,
5. organised groups,
6. organised groupings,
7. staff groups and groupings,
8. groups and groupings whose membership crosses the boundary of the centre.

Mullender (1990) gives a simpler classification:

1. group living,

2. activity groups,
3. discussion groups,
4. residents' forums,
5. authority-wide forums.

From this it is possible to say that, within a residential situation, there are groups, formed of residents, which may be permanent or transient, for example friendship groups; there are staff groups, which are mostly permanent; there are groups set up within the residence for specific purposes, comprising staff and selected residents and there are groups which involve people from outside the residence plus staff and selected residents. The aims and purposes of residential situations are very wide, in that they can range from an intense almost single purpose, as with a religious house (e.g. monastery), through establishments set up for the purposes of learning, care and custody, to treatment and change.

But whatever a residential setting is established to do, it also has the essential fact of maintenance to consider. For a residential system to be maintained in a state of functional efficiency, it will need, like all organisations, to be capable of reviewing what is happening and to base future planning on the results of that review. Any human organisational system is only as effective as the use it makes of the feedback it receives on its processes. This implies that such systems are dynamic and changing in response either to growth within, to changes in the individuals within the system (loss and replacement), or to influence and pressures from without. There is a very strong correlation between stagnation and the lack of the kind of knowledge that feedback would give and it is clear that each can be the precipitating agent of the other.

As with groups operating outside the residential setting, the primary purposes of residential groups may be either contextual or instrumental, or both. Indeed groups which are change- or treatment-oriented may well bear a very distinct resemblance to such groups held outside the residential situation, in that the main resource distribution and use is as identified earlier, in Chapter 8. As this area bears such a likeness to those already discussed it should suffice here only to note the essential differences and to concentrate on those groups and groupings which are specific to the residential situation.

The most obvious difference has already been mentioned, that selection for admission to such a group is made within the restricted population of the residential scene. Thus members of such groups already have knowledge of each other, though it may be only superficial, before entering the group, and most certainly will remain in each other's presence when each group session ends. Clarke and Aimable (1990) discuss this problem briefly in terms of 'opportunity costs'. They see one of the major obstacles to the maintenance of a selected group within a residential setting as the probability that attendance at such a group may cause the group members to 'miss out' on other, enjoyable and interesting activities available in the residential setting. This is a specific instance of the universal cost/reward analysis which applies, not just to groups and groupings, but to most, if not all, human activities. The analysis can change as perception of the rewards available in opposing or competing situations increases or decreases with experience or with change in need.

Perhaps another design factor which emerges clearly here is the need to draw a more definite distinction between group members being in the group living situation in general and being in a specific group situation with whatever focus that may have. Conversely the return from the specific group to the general residential situation may also need to be clearly signposted.

So far the emphasis has been on the focus-specific group which, apart from complexities engendered by the situation, shows little difference in design from groups with similar intent used in non-residential settings. But there is one probable factor of interest which also has some relevance in non-residential groups but which is seldom so obvious in them. This factor stems from the simple fact that selection to attend a specific group in a residential setting is a clearly visible operation to those not selected. Attendance at a group can ordinarily impose some effects upon those close to the attender, but those effects concern the relationship that one individual member has with others. In the residential setting all the members of a specific group have relationships, close or distant, with all the members of the institution: the situation is much tighter, the relationships are much more immediate and universally applicable.

The only recorded effect of this situation of which we are aware has been the concern with the development of elitism. This is simply an obvious example of a created difference, an extension of the fact that groups are inclusive operations for their members but exclusive and excluding for others. Where the informal structure of a residential situation is in marked contrast to the formal, and even more so when it is in some form of confrontation or conflict with it, this may well be a very strong obstacle to the establishment of specific focus groups within the establishment. Where difference is immediately apparent and in particular where that difference goes against the need of the sub-culture to be united and conformist, the resistance to being different can become an important factor in increasing obstacles to group development and to resource use.

When we come to consider the whole living group, perhaps the most significant design element is size. Some residential situations are small enough for the entire structure to comprise a focus-specific group without exceptions and exclusions. When this is so, the prolongation of contact time makes possible the development of a repertoire of known response patterns that much more quickly and the risk elements may be much more clearly exposed. Both these factors should also lead to the exposure of available resources and the development of their use more rapidly than in any group of similar size which meets intermittently. It is interesting in this respect that the Human Relations Laboratories in the United States were almost always conducted as residential groups with a closed membership, never very numerous, over a period of several days. Such an intense experience often produced difficulties of transferring such learning and change as was gained to the less intense and much less supportive living situation.

Large residential groups tend to be, as would be expected, containers of many smaller groups, some transient, some more permanent. Where mobility and energy factors are diminished there is often a strong tendency for individual residents to make contact with the system only at specific intervals – meal times, bed time, rising time and so on. This kind of residential situation at its lowest common denominator is a containment system which caters for the physical needs of food, shelter, warmth and the presence of others, however little regarded or used the latter may be. Thus the design element is one of an organisational nature such that those whose job it is to meet those basic physical needs are able to perform their caring functions with maximum efficiency and benefit to their residents.

The resource system in such a residential setting is markedly analogous to the extreme form of group-as-context, where the individual group leader resource is replaced by a total staff leader resource. However there are several less extreme positions possible. Breslin and Sturton (1978), describing their experimental groupwork programme in a hostel for the mentally handicapped, presented a groupwork programme for 27 residents and staff – a total residential group. This group corresponded roughly to item 4 in Brown's typology. The description is interesting in that it highlights a big problem in achieving aims for the group, namely to clarify the major obstacles, one of which was extremely illuminating and emerged only after several meetings, described by the authors as 'chaotic'. It was how to provide a model of group membership. The residents had no basic concepts of group membership which they could use. This obstacle was gradually overcome by explicit demonstration, example and role modelling. Once the residents had some behaviour to copy, the obstacle diminished and their resources became available. They became able to voice their concerns, to consider the problems of others and to help in the planning of major events which affected their lives as residents.

This was a very clear illustration of the fact of groupwork techniques being based upon the diminution or eradication of obstacles, especially as the residential group involved here was one which traditionally has been regarded as possessing few resources of its own.

> The essence of residential work thus lies, first, in the development of a 'round the clock' experience that is subjectively satisfying as well as being communally coherent, and, secondly, in the creation of opportunities for personal growth and the resolution of problems of living. (Payne, 1978, p. 60)

The design of groups in residential settings has two major aspects, those which Payne describes as 'round the clock experience' and those which are specifically designed within the total situation to deal with certain important issues. The basic group forms of instrument and context are complicated in the latter case by the number of those constituting the prime resource-providing body and by the element of size. Other special design complexities reside in the nature of the promotion of the perception of difference caused by the exclusive effect of selection in an actually enclosed population. Of course the essential purpose of the residential establishment has a great bearing upon what is feasible; for example, a totally containing institution may well be able to produce effective groups which deal with many problems, but not usually groups concerned with the basic fact of containment itself.

Two final facts which are universally applicable to all group forms but which are seen especially in residential settings are seepage and the distinct possibility that some form of preparation to recognise and use groups may be necessary. Seepage in a close community is concerned with the leakage of influence both ways through the boundaries of a constituted group. There is much evidence to indicate that the design of groups in residential settings must take cognisance of a much more potent and immediate seepage into such groups of the influence of residents who are not members of the group than can be anticipated in non-residential groups. These influences are not necessarily deleterious and may be frankly positive and good, but they emanate from a very immediate and close presence to the group. They may be concerned directly with personal safety within the system at large and thus produce a possible conflict of interests and so constitute an obstacle to commitment and to eventual resource use.

It seems to be blandly assumed that because groups are a naturally occurring phenomenon there is no real need to prepare potential members for experience within a group which may well appear to them to be an 'artificial' creation. This is particularly so with the deliberate formation of groups for specific purposes in residential situations where all too frequently the residents are not there by choice and have some suspicion of the motives of those who work in the establishment. Experience would indicate that pre-group preparation is never a waste of time even in non-residential groups, and many well-intentioned group projects have foundered because the preparedness to join and the understanding of the possible advantages of joining have been taken for granted.

10

Implications

> ... the primary requirement of a theory is that it should be *useful*. This comes even before the requirement that it should be accurate ... Theories, whether inarticulate or well worked out and backed by plenty of evidence, are primarily ways of organising experience and data. They are containers for it, which enable it to be drawn upon, applied to different situations, used, learned from and built on. The test of a good theory is therefore whether it enables us to make use of experience. (Atherton, 1986, p. 106)

The first and most important thing to consider here concerns the level at which a theory of practice exists, for it seems that there is much confusion between what actually constitutes the derived concepts of practice and any other kind of knowledge and information which might actually form the basis of action. The fundamental word in the last sentence is, of course, 'basis'. A practice theory must be derived from an understanding of what occurs when theories of behaviour are actually translated into direct action with people. There is first the general nature of such theories and the related problem of the specific nature of the direct action with actual people. But out of this can and should arise a realisation that in practice there are to be discovered processes which appear to be fundamental to all forms of groupwork and which can serve as uniting factors at a different level from general theories of behaviour, principles of practice or other idiosyncratic approaches. The concept of resource use is one of these fundamental factors; it may, indeed, be the most important one.

As was discussed earlier in this volume, the appearance of fundamental processes is fraught with problems, not least that of contamination from the motivation and expectations of practitioners, which tends to set up a simple form of self-fulfilling prophecy. It could be said that the concept of resource use is relatively free of such contamination, though, as the whole process of working with people in groups is concerned with perceptions and thus also with idiosyncratic interpretation, because it is also a process of influence, no matter how subtly and indirectly applied, contamination must assuredly exist. If, for instance, the process of a group enhances the ability of its members to perform certain social functions, the process of influence is implicit, in that someone had to have the perception at some stage that such a development was not only possible and feasible, but also compatible with those being led to make the changes. Because that 'someone' is rarely the person making the change, this is a situation in which A influences B in a way that B, while possibly ultimately accepting, had either not considered for himself or, if he had considered, had no known means of bringing about.

But this level of intervention carries with it the ethical value of being beneficial for the recipient and thus is regarded as acceptable. The essential point about the concept of resource use is that it has as part of its basis the exposure of method. Now it is by no means certain that the simple exposure of an influence makes it ethically more acceptable, but, if that process of exposure is part of the development of use and integration, the level at which understanding is produced may well be much greater. Use actually requires a level of understanding which is frequently missing in the process of simple exposure.

Another way of looking at this is to say that an extension of possible choices of behaviours which bears little or no connection to the perceived reality and experience of the individual being who is presented with it in essence constitutes no choice at all. Choice, real choice, has to be based on actual understanding of what is being offered in terms, not of the offerer, but of the person to whom such an offer is made. More importantly it should be known to the chooser what the major consequences of making that choice may be expected to be, bearing in mind that the choices available are always 'accept', 'reject', 'don't know' and conditional forms of all of these.

Of course the consequences of choice cannot be wholly or accurately predicted and, while experience may enhance predictive ability, it must be expected that unknown and random factors will influence the outcomes of any choice to some greater or lesser extent. Indeed in all forms of social intervention the most important consequences usually turn out to be those which were unforeseen, which is not anything to do with the operation of malicious fate but only the result of the insubstantial and inaccurate knowledge and data upon which the prediction was based.

It may well be that part of a realistic form of learning about groupwork should include and deal with the probability of events occurring. For, however rough these indices might prove to be, at least they would have the enormous advantage of adjusting expectation several large increments towards reality.

It is interesting that in groupwork literature little stress is placed upon ethical issues and on the concept of undue influence. Often the most that can be discovered is a consideration of some form of contract, but, as Diedrich and Dye (1972) write:

> It should be remembered that 'the contract' is not between persons who have an equal understanding of the processes involved. It cannot be assumed that the participant really knows what he is letting himself in for.

A contract is a coercive instrument if only one side to the agreement has any real knowledge of what is involved. Garvin (1981) argues that the line between coercion and urging is very fine and the difference in actual power between worker and clients (and also in the perception of power) is very great. It is also a matter of some ethical concern how workers decide between the right of the individual to choose for himself and the need to take strong measures to ensure that such an individual has a chance to find out and develop his potential.

There are no easy answers to these problems except the one usually offered, that part of the groupwork process should be the exposure not only of what is going on but also of intent. In the outcome this is *not* an easy answer either, as the problem of exposure, as we have seen, does not necessarily lead either to understanding of what is being exposed or to its acceptance.

Because the basic concepts of resource location and use go back several steps before change processes are initiated, there is probably less chance that undue influence will be exerted. As the process, most likely to be found in the instrumental form of group, is concerned with developing and using the actual and potential resources of group members, coercion in any form, explicit or covert, would have an extremely powerful tendency to be counter-productive. In the case of the group-as-instrument, the powerful position of the group leader has to be acknowledged for the group to be effective. But in either case the need for each groupworker to develop an explicit set of principles is fundamental.

The professional judgement of groupworkers is required to be exercised in another way also, when a worker is requested by an employing agency to attempt work with groups which, for one reason or another, stand little or no chance of being even moderately successful. In these circumstances everyone involved can suffer from a bad group experience. It should be part of the professional codes of practice not to enter into such situations. However it must be acknowledged that the lack of the necessary information to be able to make such a decision appropriately is often a deciding factor. But an essential part of groupwork training, which we will consider next, should focus on and develop the ability of groupworkers to assess the viability of what they are being asked to do. This implies a professional competence of a fairly high order, not so much in the actual working with the group, but in understanding the constraints and other factors which may have an effect upon it.

As has been stated many times, the unintentional and the unforeseen consequences of social intervention are often the most monumental and influential. It is not proposed that groupworkers should become seers, but it is suggested that they cultivate two things, a rational expectation level and a degree of patience and flexibility. Given that groupwork is based upon the clear understanding that it is wholly concerned with the beneficial exploitation of available and potential resources, these two factors become rather more accessible.

Where experience may have developed a groupworker's ability to assess the resources which are, or may be, available in the gestalt of group and leaders and in the available networks there should be a clearer understanding of the obstacles which impede their use. Groupwork aims are so often stated with an idealistic fervour and with a desire to be effective that the obstacles to their achievement are ignored or at least not seen in their true perspective. In any event they are not then included as the basis of a design to achieve those aims. The relationship between aims and the obstacles to them is the fundamental basis of groupwork practice. The salient point here is that, if that practice is not based upon such a relationship but upon the pursuance of an unadapted set of techniques founded upon some theoretical concepts, then the fit of work to aims and needs is at best haphazard and at worst wholly counterproductive. The whole basis of groupwork is, or should be, pragmatic, with preconditions for its use being kept to an absolute minimum, being more properly related to the known abilities and experience of the individual groupworker than to a set of ideas.

For the groupworker to realise that what he/she knows theoretically about the available resources is as clear as may be, but that the groupworker's knowledge may be only an inaccurate estimate in the area of the resources possessed by potential group members should lead to some very important planning. In the first place the resources possessed by the individual groupworker should be known with much greater clarity and precision than is usual at present. This 'knowing' should preferably be based, not upon any assumption, but upon demonstrable possession and use. To know is one thing, to know that such knowing can be, and has been, used in effective practice is entirely another. Because it may take some considerable time for the resources possessed by group members and available for use to become visible, the known ability of the groupworker to hold the group firmly until those member re-sources come on stream is essential.

This must then be accompanied by constant revision of what is possible and of the methods of using and of developing resources towards the accomplishment of such of the original goals as are possible. What emerges clearly from the concept of groupwork as the creation and use of resource systems is the idea of the current state of knowledge. So many of the probably important resource elements exist as unknowns, their very presence merely postulates based upon cumulative experience which has demonstrated such availability in the past. As with the process of maturation, where, if adequate and appropriate stimulation is not applied, and within the effective time boundaries, to young, growing creatures, the expected developmental stages are either not achieved at all or emerge in diminished or distorted form, so it is with resource development. It is also manifestly obvious that missed or bungled opportunities for development make subsequent attempts to recoup such losses very much more difficult, often incomplete and sometimes totally impossible.

The major factor of value to be derived from resource theory is a fundamental and basic simplicity which can clarify the obscurity of aim and purpose. It cannot replace other theoretical concepts of groups and groupwork, but merely offers a clear and unequivocal structure at a deeper level of organisation.

Teaching groupwork

[Teaching groupwork means showing how] to learn how to *move* in the group situation, how to develop the skills and perform the operations needed to help in groups. And I do not believe it is possible to teach these skills to social workers by placing them in groups as observers, or even by making them co-leaders with members of other disciplines. (Schwartz, 1971, p. 21)

Schwartz is most emphatic in his comments on teaching groupwork and, in our view, quite rightly so. Indeed much training for groupworkers is based upon acquiring certain well-defined techniques, whereas, in what has been implied earlier, such techniques as are used must be logically derived from the needs of a group and from the necessity to gain access to whatever resources may be available to meet those needs.

Thus the process of teaching people to work with groups should start from the earliest moment of instruction with the attempt to develop a clear understanding of why groups are used as instruments of learning, of support, change, treatment and so on. For unless this fundamental perception is in place all further learning and training will revolve around a vacuum and the tendency will almost invariably develop to replace the missing central theme with either specific techniques or with specific theoretical concepts of the ways in which people behave in group situations. This central concept of groupwork practice is simply that of the potential increase in resource availability and use which exists when a number of individuals interact co-operatively.

Groupwork training revolves around the possibility of individual workers being able to develop the necessary insights and skills to bring about that co-operative interaction. Thus a training programme can be formulated on the basis of a series of crucial questions. However there must first be a good grounding of knowledge about the ways in which people *do* act in group situations. This should be broadly and eclectically founded, and should be accepted for what it is, a combination of observation and possible explanation, with the likelihood that it can act as a guide, but above all as something which is founded on probability rather than absolute truth.

Next should come exercises to develop skill in the analysis of complex data, for it is from this kind of analysis that can arise a recognition of the possible existence of needs within a given group of people and that these needs might be met by the provision of a specifically designed group situation. For instance, some individuals may well lack information which is basic and essential to their ability to handle particular situations in their lives. The reasons for this lack may be quite varied, ranging from never having had access to the necessary information to not being able to understand it when it was offered, or not being able to use it. Thus to bring several such people into a group based upon a common need for information would be quite a logical thing to do. So the first questions which are basic to the training of groupworkers are: what are the assessed needs of the individuals under consideration and, more pertinently, how are such assessments of need made? The question which follows with absolute logic is: can these assessed needs possibly be dealt with by some form of group, given that what groups provide is access to resources?

I am often unhappy about this second question because it is frequently best preceded by another, such as: given that you have an assessment of the needs of these particular individuals, what resources will be necessary to meet them either partially or wholly? The answer to this question, if it can be given, will often decide whether there is need for a group or not. Indeed, as I have attempted to show here, a group can provide a particularly economical use of scarce specialist resources at one end of the spectrum and at the other extreme a potential resource pool formed by the abilities, knowledge and experience of the group members. The next question is: are these resources available either actually, that is here and now, or potentially? Of course answers to this question can only be based on the state of knowledge which exists at the moment of asking, which is one good and sufficient reason for all contracts to have built into them the very basic idea of renegotiation as that state of knowledge changes.

What are the perceived obstacles to these located resources being made available for use? Even if only part of the required resources is apparently available, there may still exist a large number of obstacles to their being made available for common use. But one thing is abundantly clear: that, unless obstacles are recognised and the skills of the groupworker bent to their removal or diminution, whatever potential resources they obscured will remain inaccessible. Inevitably there are obstacles which are not removable or even susceptible to being diminished or bypassed. To waste time and effort here is to detract considerably from what might be achieved by a redirection of that energy. So the next question for the learner worker is: what do you need to be able to do to eliminate or diminish the obstacles to resource access?

As we have seen, obstacles to resource access are many and varied, but it is essential that they be truly recognised for what they are, and that groupwork techniques be adapted to deal with them within the specific context of the actual group. In this context the development of methods of coping with obstacles to resource access has to be soundly based on the realities of the group situation. For instance, a technique that requires the development of an intimate level of trust must be considered in the light of the time available to the group, the experience of the group members, the skill of the worker and so on. These are the elements of group design which we have discussed in the previous chapters. Obviously actual group situations which may arise in the training sessions can be used to illustrate both the nature of obstacles to resource use and the planning of the necessary action to deal with them. But this is a far cry from creating specific examples of groupwork, such as a personal growth group. Such a process tends to inculcate a limited number of techniques, very specifically focused, which are in no sense generally applicable unless the fundamental logic of their appropriateness in the situation in which they were learned is taught as well. The lesson here is that it is the process of logical adaptation of technique to need and to the development and use of resources which is the primary factor and not the development of a limited repertoire of techniques itself.

Of course there is another side to this coin, which may be best expressed as a choice. If the acquiring of a given set of techniques is the aim of the learning situation, the field in which these techniques have a proven logical and effective use must be closely defined and that limited sphere of use accepted as irrefutable. Thus learning about groupwork is much more concerned with clarifying the relationship between needs and developing resources than with the process of acquiring techniques, because the latter, however effective they may be in the circumstances for which they were originally designed, are not and never have been universally applicable. What is universal is the need to decide with clarity what obstacles exist to resource use. Often the methods of coping are immediately suggested by that clarity of understanding. What is most apparent is that a large element of creative imagination needs to be developed in potential groupworkers so that new and explicitly focused ways of discovering and using resources become the norm, rather than the unimaginative use in all situations, whether appropriately or not, of a given number of learned techniques.

Most of this pragmatic approach to the development of resource systems can be taught by exercises which clearly specify needs and qualities and require the analysis of obstacles and of the methods of coping, together with estimates of time and other design elements. It may be an oversimplification, but if the basic logic of resource access is correctly worked out in any group, the actual practice with the group is a much easier exercise, given a reasonable degree of knowledge about group behaviour and a working sensitivity.

As the resources available to a group may comprise, in large proportion, connections outside the group, one final point about teaching groupwork needs to be made. The tendency of groupwork practitioners in the past to become so absorbed in the groups they are working with and to appear to have an interest which stops at the boundaries of those groups is a quite self-defeating process. Networks of possible resources reach a focal point in each individual member of a group and can be fed into the special network which is the group itself. Influence, bias, prejudice, knowledge and experience can all pass along these networks in both directions, in and out. Although the group may, under certain circumstances, become an encapsulating system, and this may be an essential relationship-intensifying process, most groups need access to all the resources which can be made available. To be able to develop an awareness of the presence of these networks is a required groupwork skill because, as must become clear, they will affect outcomes within the group whether they are acknowledged or not. This in turn can lead to very perplexing situations, which are very common, in which practitioners observe consequence in groups apparently without obvious cause. This phenomenon then produces responses by groupworkers, which, located as they are in ignorance of the genuine causative factors, are usually not merely ineffective but actually harmful.

Practising groupwork

Finally, social groupwork cannot be thought of as a routine technique that can be based under all circumstances in the same way and can be taught through a 'cook book' mechanical approach. It demands a practitioner who has learned to assess people and their situation, knows his or her philosophy, and has the capacity to elicit self-help forces within the individuals and groups. Then, according to their needs and capacities, he or she will develop with the group members various approaches to achieve their goals. (Konopka, 1978, p. 130)

Gisela Konopka wrote these words in a paper on the ethical value bases of groupwork, but they stand as a clear statement about both the teaching and the practice of groupwork. The paper also makes the point, which I will elaborate here, about the specific skill of group creation or adaptation in order to generate a milieu in which access to and use of resources can be elicited to meet the assessed needs of group members. The most important implication for practice from resource theory is the absolute need to understand and separate what are usually confused statements about practice. The essential groupworker skills are those which reside in the perception and assessment of need and in the creation or adaptation and maintenance of group systems. Whatever knowledge a groupworker may have about the specific needs of group members, it is analogous to the knowledge possessed by the group members.

Stated another way, the specific, different and specialist knowledge and skill of the groupworker lies in the direction of generating and maintaining group systems. Whatever other knowledge, skill and understanding a groupworker brings to the group is a bonus. This concept of 'different' skill and knowledge, while simple enough in itself and therefore obvious, has consistently been confused with and overlaid by the knowledge a groupworker may possess about the special problems of special groups of clients.

This is in no way to diminish the need for special knowledge of particular client problems, but only to put it into the general context of knowledge, experience and informational resources available to a group. There is also the distinction that must be drawn between the personal experiential knowledge of their problems, difficulties and needs which clients possess and which, although extremely pertinent, is often unstructured and almost always idiosyncratic, and the organised and structured, often impersonal and thus general knowledge and understanding of the groupworker.

The practice of groupwork is, therefore, fundamentally and essentially concerned with the creation and maintenance of groups or with the adaptation and maintenance of existing groups. The clarity with which this must be developed can be assisted by the realisation that, although the whole of human society is composed of groups in all shapes and forms, the groupworker's aim, by creation or adaptation, is to bring into existence a group of human beings as a unit system designed and maintained to exploit the resources available to it for the purpose of dealing with reasonably clearly defined needs.

Epilogue

The main thesis of this book derives from the fundamental idea that groups in many forms have been and are the principal factor in shaping and maintaining the individual. Thus, when appropriately founded, it is logical that artificial groups, that is created or adapted groups, should become the principal factors in supporting, reshaping, educating or changing the individual by use of the same system but with a greater increment of conscious intent and direction.

Following from this must come the need to know not only why groups form in the so-called natural state but, more importantly, what actually happens within those groups. Given the basic needs of human beings, the necessity of group membership is of paramount importance, but it is so universal that human beings are usually more or less unaware of their state of interdependence with others and are frequently suspicious of created groups which they regard as artificial, and there is great value placed upon the idea of individuality. But any analysis of a successful group, natural or artificial, reveals that its achievement is almost entirely dependent upon a successful matching of the group's combined and individual needs with the resources, actual and potential, to which the group has, or can gain, access.

So it would seem that the practice of groupwork is constructed around certain very basic themes, all of which in some shape or form contribute to the release and use of those resources which can most nearly be assumed to match the needs of the group at a given time. For the groupworker this implies an ability to recognise need plus the skill to convene and hold a group together while the appropriate available resources are made visible and to ensure their take-up and use.

The process of planning or designing a group may be either a long-term and very careful process, taking full cognisance of all the factors known at the time of design, or an instantaneous decision brought about to meet an immediately developing need. But by far the most important part of groupwork lies in what is done to bring about changes in perception. Most of life is lived on what may be described as 'automatic pilot', where traditional responses are triggered by familiar cues and no great amount of conscious thought goes into the process. This reduces the overall expenditure of consideration and probably leaves more energy available to tackle all those problems which are new or different. When life runs with a degree of smoothness or is in a relatively static state this is an obvious advantage. Habitual responses are fine when they are all that is required or when they are well designed and adaptive.

However, when situations cease to be usual, or the response becomes cumulatively maladaptive, then help may be required to bring about a shift both in understanding and in response. We have discussed these facts as obstacles to resource use and postulated that the most effective way to deal with most obstacles which are preventing the changes just noted from occurring is, first, to explore their existence and consequences and, second, to show that alternatives exist. This demonstration should take place, not so much as information, though that may be essential, but as the practice of other individuals of similar nature and in similar situations.

By far the most important of all obstacles to resource use may well be the restricted boundaries of the way individuals think about their abilities to cope and of their belief in the existence of viable alternatives. This is most clearly stated in the acceptance by the helping professions that an actual change of situation or a change of perception of the nature of that situation, or some combination of both, are all the approaches that exist. In essence this boils down to a matter of attempting to increase the number of compatible and available choices.

A major problem about this has always been that groupworkers have a strong tendency to believe that the resources they themselves bring to a group are the most important ones. Of course, in a very clear and simple way this is true, providing their resource bringing is comprised of the skills of matching needs and of holding a group together until the member resource pool can be located and made visible. The skills of the groupworker reside in the ability to recognise need and to guide the creation or adaptation of a structure or system in which the use of appropriate resources is not only possible but beneficially effective. This is fundamentally true of all forms of groupwork, from the transient grouping to the long-term group, from support activities to treatment and from leader-resourced groups to group-resourced groups.

Perhaps the use of such a term as 'resource-use' has a harsh economic sound, but in essence the hardness is necessary to define the basic essentials. Hirschman and Lindblom (1962), in a discussion about systems theory, use the term 'resource mobilisation', which appears to define quite accurately what groupwork is about. It is of little consequence where the resource is located, but of paramount importance that it be appropriate to the need and mobilised for use.

Given Haskell's (1975) strictures on the hidden influences at work in groups, the powers which reside in leaders, the influence of the past and other underminers of objectivity and value-free approaches, resources, their location and use must be the only *rational* approach: rational because such an approach implies that knowledge of the existence of influence systems and their possible consequences is included in it; rational because, given that resource discovery and use are the ultimate aims, skill is deployed logically to remove or diminish obstacles to these resources and to their use for the maximum possible benefit for the group. Thus open and conscious use of influence systems replaces the covert way in which they are usually employed and a large increment of reality is built into the approach.

'Empowerment' is a term much used and, equally, much misused, for it implies a process of giving whereas, as far as power is concerned, what actually happens in a transfer of power is that perceptions change according to a recognition of the bases upon which power rests. As long as empowerment is not held as an article of faith but as a necessary partial redistribution based on a change of perception, lack of influence and power being a major obstacle to the recognition and use of resources, it is a process very closely tied to reality.

The idea of partial redistribution may seem grudging to some, but as Lang (1972) has shown circumstances have often generated people who need a gradual access to influence and power and most certainly need guidance in their use. Some, indeed, need power to reside in the hands of others who are regarded (on the basis of observation) as safe until they can develop the capacity to handle at least some of that influence themselves.

The practice of groupwork is an exercise in the co-operative discovery and use of resources for the mutual benefit of all group members.

References

1 Introduction

Andreski, S. (1974) *Social Sciences as Sorcery* (Harmondsworth, Penguin).

Blanton, R. (1962) 'Science and Art in the Training of Psychologists', *Journal of Clinical Psychology*, vol. 8, p. 10.

Bolton, N. (1976) *The Psychology of Thinking* (London, Methuen).

Boyd, R. D. (1991) *Personal Transformation in Small Groups: a Jungian Perspective* (London and New York, Tavistock/Routledge).

Cartwright, D. and A. Zander (1953) *Group Dynamics: Research and Theory* (London, Tavistock).

CCETSW (1976) *Values in Social Work*, paper 13, London.

Garvin, C. D. (1981) *Contemporary Groupwork* (Englewood Cliffs, NJ, Prentice-Hall).

Kadushin, A. (1959) 'The Knowledge Base of Social Work', in A. J. Kahn (ed.), *Issues in American Social Work* (New York, Columbia University Press) pp. 39–79.

McCleod, D. L. and H. J. Meyer (1967) 'A Study of the Values of Social Workers', in E. Thomas (ed.), *Behavioral Science for Social Workers* (New York, Free Press) pp. 401–16.

Pappell, C. P. and B. Rothman (1966) 'Social Groupwork Models: Possession and Heritage', *Journal of Education for Social Work*, 2(2) pp. 66–77.

Pashley, B. W. (1967) 'Social Work Models', *Social Work*, 24(4) pp. 12–17.

Rosenthal, W. A. (1973) 'Social Group Work Theory', *Social Work*, 18(5) pp. 60–6.

Schwartz, W. (1963) 'Small Group Science and Groupwork Practice', *Social Work*, 8(4) pp. 39–46.

Silverman, M. (1966) 'Knowledge in Social Group Work: a Review of the Literature', *Social Work*, 11(3) pp. 56–62.

Timms, N. (1959) 'Theory and Practice in Social Work Education', *Case Conference*, 5(7) pp. 167–73.

Wilson, G. (1956) 'Social Groupwork Theory and Practice', in *The Social*

Welfare Forum, Proceedings of the National Conference on Social Welfare (New York, Columbia University Press) p. 150.

2 Interactive and affiliative patterns in groups

Aronson, E. (1980) *The Social Animal*, 3rd edn (San Francisco, H. Freeman and Company) p. 1.
Bonner, H. (1959) *Group Dynamics: Principles and Applications* (New York, The Ronald Press Co.) p. 46.
Dru, A. (1938) *The Journals of Kierkegaard, 1834/1854* (London, Oxford University Press).
Henriques, J., W. Holloway, C. Urwin, C. Venn and V. Walkerdine (1984) *Changing the Subject* (London, Methuen) p. 13.
Israel, J. (1956) *Self Evaluation and Rejection in Groups* (Uppsala, Almaquist & Wicksell) pp. 121 ff.
Jackson, J. M. (1953) 'Reference Group Processes in Formal Organisations', in D. Cartwright and A. Zander (eds), *Group Dynamics: Research and Theory* (London, Tavistock).
Malinowski, B. (1939) *The American Journal of Sociology*, May, pp. 936–46.
Raven, B. H. and J. Z. Rubin (1976) *Social Psychology: People in Groups* (New York, John Wiley) pp. 41–55.
Sherif, C. W. (1976) *Orientation in Social Psychology* (New York, Harper & Row), pp. 201–3.
Stogdill, R. M. (1959) *Individual Behaviour and Group Achievement* (New York, Oxford University Press), p. 18.
Zalesnik, A. and D. Moment (1964) *The Dynamics of Interpersonal Behaviour* (New York, John Wiley) pp. 66–95.
Zander, A. and A. Havelin (1960) 'Social Comparison and Intergroup Attraction', *Human Relations,* 13, pp. 21–32.

3 Associative patterns in created and adapted groups

Argyle, M. (1970) *Social Interaction* (London, Methuen).
Bruno, F. J. (1957) *Trends in Social Work 1874–1956* (New York, Columbia University Press).
Cartwright, D. and A. Zander (1953) *Group Dynamics: Research and Theory* (London, Tavistock).
Collins, B. E. and H. Guetzkow (1964) *A Social Psychology of Group Processes for Decision-making* (New York, John Wiley).
Gordon, T. (1972) 'A description of the Group Centred Leader', in R. C. Diedrich and H. A. Dye (eds), *Group Procedures; Purposes, Processes and Outcomes* (Boston, Houghton Mifflin) pp. 71–101.
Haskell, R. E. (1975) 'The Presumptions of Groupwork: a value analysis', *Small Group Behavior, 6(4)* (London, Sage Publications).

Janis, I. L. (1972) *Victims of Groupthink: a psychological study of foreign policy decisions and fiascoes* (Boston, Houghton Mifflin).

Katz, D. and R. L. Kahn (1969) 'Common Characteristics of Open Systems', in F. E. Emery (ed.), *Systems Thinking* (Harmondsworth, Penguin).

Lang, N. C. (1972) 'A Broad-range Model of Practice in the Social Work Group', *Social Service Review*, 46(1) pp. 76–89.

Lang, N. C. (1973) 'The Selection of the Small Group for Service Delivery: An exploration of the literature on group use in social work', *Social Work with Groups*, 1(3) (New York, Haworth Press) pp. 247–63.

Northen, H. (1987) 'Selection of Groups as the Preferred Modality of Practice', in J. Lassner, K. Powell and E. Finnegan (eds), Social Group-work: Competence and Values in Practice (New York, Haworth Press).

Raven, B. H. and J. Z. Rubin (1976) *Social Psychology: People in Groups* (New York, John Wiley).

Rosenthal, W. A. (1970) 'A Theory of Beginnings in Social Group Work Process', unpublished doctoral dissertation, Pennsylvania School of Social Work, April.

Smith, D. (1978) 'Dyadic Encounter: The Foundation of Dialogue and the Group Process', *Small Group Behavior*, 9(2) (London, Sage Publications) pp. 287–304.

Toffler, A. (1970) *Future Shock* (London, Pan).

4 Resources

Collins, B. E. and H. Guetzkow (1964) *A Social Psychology of Group Processes for Decision-making* (New York, John Wiley).

Miller, G. A. (1969) *The Psychology of Communication* (Harmondsworth, Penguin).

Napier, R. N. and M. K. Gershenfeld (1973) *Groups: Theory and Experience* (Boston, Houghton Mifflin).

Reed, Langford *The Limerick Book*.

Schumacher, E. F. (1974) *Small is Beautiful* (London, Abacus).

Shaw, J. (1974) *The Self in Social Work* (London, Routledge & Kegan Paul).

Strickler, M. and J. Allgeyer (1967) 'The Crisis Group: A New Application of Crisis Theory', *Social Work*, 12(3) July.

Thomas, S. E. (1975) *Economics* (London, English University Press).

Wilden, A. (1980) *System and Culture* (London, Tavistock) p. 21 (quoting J. Lacan, 1956).

5 Obstacles

Bass, B. M. and G. Dunteman (1963) 'Behavior in groups as a function of self-interaction, and task orientation', *Journal of Abnormal & Social Psychology,* 66, pp. 419–28.

Benne, K. D., L. P. Bradford and R. Lippitt (1964), in L. P. Bradford, J. R. Gibb and K. D. Benne (eds), *T. Group Theory and Laboratory Method* (New York, John Wiley).

Brehm, J. W. (1966) *A Theory of Psychological Reactance* (New York, Academic Press).

Collins, B. E. and H. Guetzkow (1964) *A Social Psychology of Group Processes for Decision Making* (New York, John Wiley).

Davis, J. H. (1969) *Group Performance* (Reading, Mass., Addison-Wesley).

Deutsch, M. (1988) 'Trust and Suspicion', *Journal of Conflict Resolution*, 2, pp. 265–79.

Ford, D. L., P. M. Nemiroff and W. A. Pasmore (1977) 'Group Decision-making Performance as Influenced by Group Tradition', *Small Group Behavior*, *8(2)* (London, Sage Publications).

Gibb, J. R. (1964) 'Climate for Trust Formation', in L. P. Bradford, J. R. Gibb and K. D. Benne (eds), *T. Group Theory and Laboratory Method* (New York, John Wiley) pp. 279–309.

Glover, J. A. and T. Chambers (1978) 'The Creative Production of the Group: Effects of Small Group Structure', *Small Group Behavior 9(3)*, (London, Sage Publications) pp. 387–92.

Goldbart, S. and L. Cooper (1976) 'Safety in Groups: An Existential Analysis', *Small Group Behavior*, *7(2)* (London, Sage Publications) pp. 237 ff.

Hoffman, L. R. (1965) 'Group Problem-Solving', in L. Berkowitz (ed.), *Advances in Experimental Psychology* (London, Academic Press) vol. II, pp. 99–132.

Jones, E. E. and R. E. Nisbett (1971) *The Actor and the Observer: Divergent Perceptions of the Causes of Behavior* (Morristown, NJ, General Learning Press).

McGrath, J. I. and I. Altman (1966) *Small Group Research* (New York, Holt, Rinehart).

Melnick, J. and G. S. Rose (1979) 'Expectancy and Risk-Taking Propensity: Prediction of Group Performance', *Small Group Behavior*, *10(3)* (London, Sage Publications).

Rosenberg, M. J. (1956) 'Cognitive Structure and Attitudinal Effect', *Journal of Abnormal & Social Psychology*, 53, pp. 367–72.

Schwartz, W. (1971) 'On the Use of Groups in Social Work Practice', in W. Schwartz and S. P. Zalba (eds), *The Practice of Groupwork* (New York, Columbia University Press) pp. 3–24.

Stock, D. (1964) 'A survey of research on T. Groups', in L. P. Bradford, J. R. Gibb and K. D. Benne (eds), *T. Group Theory and Laboratory Method* (New York, John Wiley) pp. 395–441.

6   Techniques that groupworkers Use

Bales, R. F. (1950) 'A Set of Categories for the Analysis of Small Group Interaction', *American Sociological Review,* 15.

Bertcher, H. J. (1979) *Group Participation: Techniques for Leaders and Members* (London, Sage Publications).

Garvin, C. D. (1981) *Contemporary Groupwork* (Englewood Cliffs, NJ, Prentice-Hall).

Heap, K. (1985) *The Practice of Social Work with Groups: a systematic approach*, National Institute Social Services Library No. 49 (London, George Allen & Unwin).

Hodge, J. (1979) 'Social Groupwork – rules for establishing the group', *Social Work Today*, 8(17) pp. 8–11.

Klein, A. F. (1972) *Effective Groupwork* (New York, Association Press).

Lerner, B. (1972) *Therapy in the Ghetto: Political Impotence and Personal Disintegration* (Baltimore, Johns Hopkins Press) p. 11.

Manor, O. (1988) 'Preparing the Client for Social Groupwork: An Illustrated Framework', *Groupwork*, *1(2)* (London, Whiting & Birch) pp. 100–14.

Mullender, A. and D. Ward (1989) 'Challenging Familiar Assumptions: Preparing for and Initiating a Self-directed Group', *Groupwork*, *2(1)* (London, Whiting & Birch) pp. 5–26.

Scheidlinger, S. (1953) 'The Concept of Social Groupwork and of Group Psychotherapy', *Social Casework,* 34.

Schwartz, W. (1971) 'On the Use of Groups in Social Work Practice', in W. Schwartz and S. P. Zalba (eds), *The Practice of Groupwork* (New York, Columbia University Press).

Toren, N. (1972) *Social Work: The Case of a Semi-profession* (Beverly Hills, Sage Publications).

7 Resource theory

Coffey, H. S. (1952) 'Socio and Psyche Group Process: Integrative Concepts', *Journal of Social Issues,* 8.

Collins, B. E. and H. Guetzkow (1964) *A Social Psychology of Group Processes for Decision Making* (New York, John Wiley).

Kendall, M. G. (1961) 'Natural Law in the Social Services', *Journal of the Royal Statistical Society,* vol. 124, part 1, pp. 1–16.

Lang, N. C. (1978) 'The Selection of the Small Group for Service Delivery: an exploration of the literature on group use in social work', in *Social Work with Groups, 1(3)* (New York, Haworth Press) pp. 247–64.

Toren, N. (1972) *Social Work: The Case of a Semi-profession* (Beverly Hills, Sage Publications).

8 Group design I

Dewey, J. (1938) *Experience and Education* (New York, Collier Books).

Engebrigsten, G. K. and K. Heap (1988) 'Short Term Groupwork in the Treatment of Chronic Sorrow', in *Groupwork, 1(3)* (London, Whiting & Birch) pp. 197–214.

Feldman, R. A. and J. S. Wodarski (1975) *Contemporary Approaches to Group Treatment* (London, Jossey Bass).

Klein, J. G. (1961) 'Social Group Treatment: some selected dynamics', in *New Perspectives on Services to Groups* (New York, National Association of Social Workers) pp. 35–47.

Kurland, R. (1978) 'Planning: the Neglected Component of Group Development', in *Social Work with Groups, 1(2)* (New York, Haworth Press) pp. 173–8.

Lang, N. C. (1972) 'A Broad-range Model of Practice in the Social Work Group', *Social Service Review*, 46(1) pp. 76–89.

Miller, G. A. (1969) 'Psychology as a Means of Promoting Human Welfare', *American Psychologist*, pp. 1064–74.

Pappell, C. P. and B. Rothman (1966) 'Social Groupwork Models Possession and Heritage', *Journal of Education for Social Work,* 2(2) pp. 66–77.

Torras, A. C. (1989/90) 'Family Group Treatment in Drug Abuse', in *Groupwork, 2(3)* (London, Whiting & Birch) pp. 257–62.

9   Group design II

Breslin, A. and S. Sturton (1978) 'Groupwork in a Hostel for Mentally Handicapped', in N. McCaughan (ed.), *Groupwork: Learning and Practice*, National Institute Social Services Library No. 33 (London, George Allen & Unwin).

Brown, A. (1990) 'Groupwork with a Difference: The group "mosaic" in residential and day care settings', in *Groupwork, 3(3)* (London, Whiting & Birch) pp. 269–85.

Clarke, P. and A. Aimable (1990) 'Groupwork Techniques in a Residential Primary School for Educationally Disturbed Boys', in *Groupwork, 3(1)* (London, Whiting & Birch) pp. 36–48.

Douglas, T. (1978) *Basic Groupwork* (London, Tavistock).

Garvin, C. D. (1981) *Contemporary Groupwork* (Englewood Cliffs, NJ, Prentice-Hall).

Levy, L. H. (1976) 'Self-help: Types of Psychological Processes', *Journal of Applied Behavioral Science,* 12, pp. 310–22.

Matzat, J. (1989/90) 'Self-help Groups as Basic Care in Psychotherapy and Social Work', in *Groupwork, 3(2)* (London, Whiting & Birch) pp. 248–56.

Mullender, A. (1990) 'Groupwork in Residential Settings for Elderly People', in *Groupwork, 3(3)* (London, Whiting & Birch) pp. 286–301.

Payne, C. (1978) 'Working with Groups in a Residential Setting', in N. McCaughan (ed.), *Groupwork: Learning and Practice*, National Institute Social Services Library, no. 33 (London, George Allen & Unwin) pp. 58–70.

Priestley, P., J. McGuire, D. Flegg, V. Hemsley and D. Welham (1978) *Social Skills and Personal Problem Solving: a handbook of methods* (London, Tavistock).

Robinson, D. (1977) 'The Lord helps those. . .', *Community Care,* Feb. pp. 16–17.
Robinson, D. (1980) 'Self Help Health Groups', in P. B. Smith (ed.), *Small Groups and Personal Change* (London, Methuen) chap. 7.

10 Implications

Atherton, J. S. (1986) *Professional Supervision in Group Care* (London, Tavistock).
Diedrich, R. C. and H. A. Dye (eds) (1972) *Group Procedures: Purposes, Processes and Outcomes* (Boston, Houghton Mifflin).
Garvin, C.D. (1981) *Contemporary Groupwork* (Englewood Cliffs, NJ, Prentice-Hall).
Konopka, G. (1978) 'The Significance of Social Groupwork Based on Ethical Values', in *Social Work with Groups, 1(2)* (New York, Haworth Press) pp. 123–32.
Schwartz, W. (1971) 'On the use of Groups in Social Work Practice', in W. Schwartz and S. P. Zalba (eds), *The Practice of Groupwork* (New York, Columbia University Press).

Epilogue

Haskell, R. E. (1975) 'Presumptions of Groupwork: A Value Analysis', *Small Group Behavior, 6(4)* (London, Sage Publications) pp. 469–86.
Hirschman, A. O. and C. E. Lindblom (1962) 'Economic Development, Research and Development, Policy Making: Some Converging Views', in P. E. Emery (ed.), *Systems Thinking* (Harmondsworth, Penguin) pp. 351–71.
Lang, N. C. (1972) 'A Broad-range Model of Practice in the Social Work Group', *Social Service Review,* 46(1) pp. 76–89.

Index